DIVINE PARADOXES

DIVINE
PARADOXES

A Finite View
of an
Infinite God

A RESPONSE TO
PROCESS AND OPENNESS THEOLOGIES

Jon Tal Murphree

Christian Publications
CAMP HILL, PENNSYLVANIA

Christian Publications, Inc.
3825 Hartzdale Drive, Camp Hill, PA 17011
www.cpi-horizon.com

Faithful, biblical publishing since 1883

ISBN: 0-87509-771-5

Contents

Introduction 1

1. Surveying the Terrain 5

2. Eternality and Temporality 15

3. Timelessness and Temporal Experience 23

4. Foreknowledge and Contingency 35

5. Omniscience and Non-consciousness 49

6. Omnipotence and Limitations 57

7. Sovereignty and Freedom 69

8. Libertarianism and Its Implications 81

9. Transcendence and Omnipresence 89

10. Constancy and Changeableness 99

11. Independence and Relationality 109

12. Impassibility and Affectability 119

13. Object of Worship and Interactive Friend ... 131

Notes 135

Introduction

From the time of the early Church fathers throughout the Middle Ages, philosophy was the handmaid of religion. Dogmatics was defended by apologetics, and faith was not separated from reason.

Then came the Enlightenment, which drove a wedge between reason and faith, lifting up reason as the sole authority.

Reacting against this extreme rationalism, religious existentialism opted for the heart over the head. Søren Kierkegaard advocated bypassing rationality with a "blind leap" of faith. Karl Barth urged on his followers what he called "irrational faith." Head-over-heart posture was inverted to heart-over-head. Religion became esoteric, divorced from reason, preserving the cleavage.

For practical purposes, human activity did not need to be aligned with the theological. Life was not integrated. Rational truth was not in a position to direct life. We could remain formal religionists while being practical secularists. Even non-religionists came to regard faith as functionally valuable, but with no basis in truth.

Being thinking creatures, however, we were not comfortable with this arbitrary construct. To accommodate our rational inclinations, we kept answering Tertullian's question in the affirmative—Athens *does* have something to do with Jerusalem. Either we had to conform heart to head or head to heart. Then we discovered how much less demanding it is to adjust our views than conform our lives. We banked on Dietrich

Bonhoeffer and Harvey Cox to give theological rationale for secular lifestyles.

While secular theology resolved our rational needs, it overlooked our human religious propensities. Being incurably religious, we were left rootless and insecure. Our impoverished spirits kept drifting back toward God. But without objective theological guidelines, we began looking for a user-friendly God, for religious truth based on functionality, for a theology derived from human experience.

This opened the door, on the one hand, for a man-centered theology of Christian experience, more anthropological than theological, appropriating social sciences through pop psychologists and liberationists under the umbrella of the Christian religion. "God is a good friend to have" became the mood of the Church.

On the other hand, the contemporary spiritual quest without theological authority has made our culture vulnerable to neo-paganism. Today we have before us a smorgasbord of bizarre religious and quasi-religious systems; many are grounded in Eastern mysticism, such as Zen Buddhism, transcendental meditation and New Age.

Western culture has been infected with a plethora of pagan viruses, and the only antibiotic is a rational theology that meets spiritual needs. Termites have weakened our theological foundations. We desperately need a theology of God that accommodates both our rational and religious needs. Reason and faith must complement each other; head and heart must be integrated.

A recent resurgence of theological literature about God is refreshing, but the rising controversy over the concept of God needs to be addressed. Because most valid Christian theology follows from the theology of God, an incorrect or inadequate view of God alters every other area. A Liberal[1] view of God's holiness, for instance, resulted in a weak theology of sin, which produced a weak theology of the atonement. A sentimental interpretation of God's love led to antinomianism and moral softness. One's view of divine sovereignty alters one's view of human freedom and moral responsibility.

Of all areas of academic inquiry, the theology of God should demand the most intellectual caution—a caution to be shared by scholar, teacher and preacher. A.W. Tozer said, "It is morally imperative that we purge from our minds all ignoble concepts of the Deity."[2]

With apologies to Charles Hartshorne, Clark Pinnock and others, I am positioning this study in the debate sparked by Process theology and what has recently been called Free Will Theism or Openness theology. In the introduction to *The Openness of God*, Pinnock and his contributors state, "We know that our arguments are open to question, and we welcome the discussion we hope they will generate."[3] It is in response to their magnanimous generosity that I enter the discussion. In many areas we will agree. Areas of disagreement will be stated in the spirit of Christian fraternity, academic debate and prudent caution.

While I appreciate the practical conclusions of the Openness proponents, I propose that they have sacrificed much more about God than is necessary for their conclusions. Indeed, much of what they sacrifice needs to be retained and reaffirmed in order to strengthen their conclusions.

Though my treatment of divine paradoxes rides piggyback on the attention given to Openness theology, Pinnock's book is not prerequisite reading. Since this volume carries the paradoxes beyond the scope of Openness, it should not be considered exclusively a response to *The Openness of God*. It is not primarily a polemic against Process and Openness theologies. Rather it is a positive study of the controversial areas about God that these theologies have raised. And it contains a built-in corrective to what I consider to be extremes in both Process theism and the model of God depicted by Openness theology.

The book is presented as a serious but not exhaustive work for clergy, students and theologically literate laypersons. The purpose is to help solidify our theological foundations, to give a rational basis for religious experience and to contribute to the restructuring of fractured relationships with God.

Chapter 1

Surveying the Terrain

When Greg got the idea that God was a tyrant, he wisely made every effort to avoid offending Him. His friend Todd, however, got the notion that God was a pushover, so he tried to manipulate Him for favors. Though sadly misinformed about God's nature, they both were correct in attempting to relate to God within the context of what He is like.

Two heavy-duty questions stand at the core of Christian theology, questions that most world systems have wrestled with: What is God like? and, How does God relate to the world and mankind? One question is substantive, the other relational. Of the two, the first is more important, because its answer determines the answer to the second. What God does is specified to a degree by what He is, and the way He relates is defined by what He is like.

The adherents of most religions attempt to relate to their god(s) within this same context. It would be improper to approach a powerful God with arrogance, a loving God with hostility or a holy God with a super-secular attitude. We cannot relate to a wise, omniscient God deceptively, nor to an authoritative God rebelliously. It would not be appropriate to approach a distant deity expecting closeness or a divine robot expecting personal response.

Discovering What God Is Like

Since relating to God is both the most important activity and the most meaningful experience of life, knowing what God is like is the most worthy propositional knowledge we will ever acquire. Is God harsh or gentle, wise or foolish, distant or close, demanding or indulgent, strong or weak, disciplined or impulsive? Is He stable or fickle, moralistic or sentimental, mechanical or personal, eternal or temporal, infinite or finite, determinative or determined? These are heavyweight matters.

An Old Testament character asked rhetorically, "Can you discover the depths of God? Can you discover the limits of the Almighty?" (Job 11:7). Human rationality alone cannot reason to what God is like, simply because human reason cannot supply the premises from which to reason.

Fortunately for us, however, God has given some information about Himself that He obviously wanted us to know. This we call revelation. The Bible is specific in some of its pronouncements about God. Additionally He has supplied some premises both in nature and in biblical revelation from which we can deduce certain conclusions about God. God has taken the initiative in communicating to us either directly or indirectly some propositions about Himself that are important for us to know.

Certainly, even in eternity, we will never be in a position to access everything about God. He has left us in the dark about many things. Certain items about Him are beyond human ability to conceive. You cannot pour all of God into a finite mind any more than you can pour all the ocean into a coffee cup. But even our inability to fully comprehend Him communicates to us something about God, that He is bigger and richer and probably more beautiful than we can surmise. We can never download all of God to our human hard drive.

Questionable Views

From the time of the early Church fathers certain propositions about God have been generally held, though never with full consensus among theologians. Generally agreed upon, however, have been such notions as the eternality of God, His foreknowledge, transcendence, sovereignty, independence, immutability (with less agreement about His impassibility) and a host of other items, some of which have been questioned by Process and Openness theologies.

Just as some Wesleyans have become more Wesleyan than Wesley himself, some in the Calvinist tradition have been more Calvinistic than Calvin. Seventeenth-century theologians such as Francis Turretin[1] and William Ames[2] developed extreme interpretations of Calvin's views. The radical doctrine of supralapsarianism (that God decreed the human moral fall), for instance, has been identified with Calvinism, though it was developed by Theodore Beza, who represented a strong movement toward hyper-Calvinism. But his brand of theology was generally rejected by Calvinists.[3] Perhaps it was the residual traces of these extreme views that John Greenleaf Whittier denounced as "iron creeds."[4]

Two contemporary theological systems, Process and Openness, have stereotyped the mainstream of traditional theology in that inflexible mode of hyper-Calvinism.

Process theologians chose the phrase "classical theism" as a label for a rigid interpretation of God's immutability and used it as a point of departure to justify Process theism. Commenting on this stereotype created by Process theologians, David Burrell says, "The God which emerges is unresponsive and aloof . . . hardly fit for Christian worship." He admits that "such a God has been all too familiar to Western consciousness" but he denies that it represents the mainstream of historic Christianity.[5]

Process reaction to the perceived rigid theological position of "classical theism" has been enunciated by theologians such as Charles Hartshorne, John Cobb and Schubert Ogden. Based on Whiteheadian process metaphysics, Process theology offers a God who is immanent but not transcendent, finite rather than infinite, a part of the system rather than above the system. Constantly in the process of actualizing his potential, God is interdependent with the world, without self-fulfillment, limited in power.

Process theology's appeal consists in making God interactive with humankind. He is caring and compassionate, capable of being both hurt and pleased, not responsible for permitting evil simply because He is not able to prevent evil and is constantly updating Himself to be relevant to a changing culture. God exercises His limited power by persuasion rather than by force and He leads by consensus and cooperation rather than autocracy.

Similarly, Openness theology identifies mainstream historic theology with the most extreme views of a broader Calvinism. Representing the Openness position Richard Rice writes:

> For most of Christian history, one idea of God and his relation to the world has dominated the church's perspective. . . . In this perspective . . . God is equally glorified and his purposes are equally well served by the obedience of the righteous, the rebellion of sinners, the redemption of the saints and the destruction of the wicked. . . . He is untouched by the disappointments, sorrow and suffering of his creatures.[6]

From this perspective, Clark H. Pinnock and his contributors to *The Openness of God*[7] are concerned that traditional theology does not logically allow the kind of loving, caring, responsive, interactive God the Judeo-Christian Scriptures depict and the kind of fellowship with God the Church has generally practiced. They recognize the modern cultural mood to respond to an interactive God for fellowship rather than a passive God simply to worship and they think the Bible presents an interactive God.

Pinnock speaks of "the living God who is metaphysically social." He says,

> God is one whose ways are marked by flexibility and dynamism, who acts and reacts on behalf of his people, who does not exist in splendid isolation from the world of change, but relates to his creatures. . . . God not only directs but interacts. No unmoved mover, God responds sensitively to what happens on earth and relates to us. God is the omnipotent Creator but exercises his power subtly and carefully in the world. By bringing other free agents into being and entering into their lives in love, God is open.[8]

A Cursory Critique

A few preliminary statements are in order.

First, while the Openness theologies are in serious error at points, proponents of Openness have correctly understood the Christian God as a relational God, dynamic rather than static, interactive rather than passive, loving and caring rather than cold and indifferent, the kind of God that elicits positive human response. On almost every page of the Bible, God "comes through" as concerned, responsive and caring. This scripturally correct model of God provides both the rationale and the climate for relating to God meaningfully.

Second, proponents of Openness portray mainstream orthodox theology as being in the rigid theological mold, subscribing to an inflexible God who is set in concrete, unaffected by human suffering, and whose foreknowledge precludes any

measure of human freedom. Though Openness makes conces-
sions to a few theologians who were somewhat broader, most
of historical theology is accused of logically leaving no place
for a caring, relational God who is active on the temporal level.
And that view of God is labeled "classical theology." This strikes
me as a simplistic and unfair categorization.

Neo-Calvinist theologians as well as moderate Arminians
have defined theologies of God that are at once consistent and
broad enough to accommodate divine-human relationships.
Over a century ago the notion of Openness was emphasized
by classical Liberalism, without using the term, almost to the
point of humanizing God. Excesses of Liberalism were cor-
rected by a Barthian dialectical theology that reemphasized the
infinity, transcendence and holiness of God but left adequate
room for a personal existential encounter with God. Pushing
traditional mainstream theology into a narrow hyper-Calvinism
to make room for a relational model of God smacks of a "straw
man" fallacy. Rigid immutability is not the only model of God
that is deep in classical tradition. To present two models of
God—the "traditional" and the relational—is to set up a false
dichotomy.

Third, Openness theologians insist that much of the traditional view of God came from Greek philosophy rather than
the Bible. Then, with some modifications and disclaimers, they
argue against the traditional view on the grounds that it derived from Hellenistic philosophy. Later I will cite scriptural
support for some of the ideas they attribute to the Greeks and
suggest the Church fathers may have arrived independently
at some of the same conclusions about God.

Even if Openness theologians are correct that elements of
Christian theology are derived from Hellenism, arguing
against a position because of its origin does not invalidate the
position. In logic this move is called the genetic fallacy. To
suggest a view is wrong because it came from philosophy is to

do a sleight of hand. It omits an important step in the deduction. The argument requires an intermediate proposition stating that philosophy is wrong, but that proposition is only assumed in the Openness argument—not stated.

Arriving at a conclusion philosophically does not of itself falsify the conclusion. Nor should it be considered false because it was held by ancient Greek philosophers or medieval Latin theologians. Certainly we should draw no final conclusions from speculative philosophy, though Plato, Aristotle, Anselm and Aquinas were analytic philosophers and deserve the highest of academic respect. A Hebrew psalmist suggested that God has placed premises in nature from which some propositions about God may be deduced even by the pagan:

> The heavens are telling of the glory of God;
> And their expanse is declaring the work of His hands.
> Day to day pours forth speech,
> And night to night reveals knowledge. . . .
> Their line has gone out through all the earth,
> And their utterances to the end of the world.
>   (Psalm 19:1-4)

The Openness View

Advocates of Openness correctly insist that some extreme views of God need to be rethought in a biblical light, and some of the rigid definitions need to be redone.

None of the terms that describe God should be used in an undisciplined, unqualified way. Those who insist that the terms are absolute often overlook the fact that they can only be absolute in the areas to which they apply. For instance, one cannot say that God is unlimited without specifying what area is unlimited, because being unlimited in one area often necessitates limitations in another. If God is unlimited in goodness, that alone means He is limited in badness. If He is unlimited in

11

power He is automatically limited from weakness—by His unlimited power. God cannot be perfect in every area, for to be perfect in knowledge means He is not perfectly ignorant.[9]

Irrationality poses no particular problems for Neo-Orthodoxy, based on Barth's "irrational faith," which attempts to arrive at truth existentially. Post-liberal theology admittedly abandons rational categories, attempting to achieve functional experience rather than to arrive at objective truth.

Charles Hartshorne claims his Process theology is rational, but much of it is open to question. In what he calls "Divine Relativity," Hartshorne combines in God all polar opposites in ways that seem to be contradictory—perfection and imperfection, absoluteness and relativity, eternality and changeableness, being creator and created, abstract and concrete, independent and dependent, necessary and contingent.[10] Because God is all-inclusive, Hartshorne claims, He embraces mutual exclusives. What appears to be a conglomerate contradiction is defended in the name of a higher rationality.

Openness proponents, on the other hand, commendably reject what is logically contradictory. They reject divine polarities that are often justified in the name of mystery or paradox. What concerns me, however, is that Openness has rejected such traditional notions as the timelessness and the direct foreknowledge of God and watered down the notions of sovereignty and immutability—all on rational grounds, assuming these traditional notions do not allow for the biblical God who is involved in time, who grants freedom to His subjects and allows human input into His activities. Though Openness has not abandoned such notions as the majesty, holiness and power of God, I contend it has unnecessarily modified some of the traditional concepts. Advocates of Openness have sacrificed more than is rationally necessary to have the dynamic, relational, affectable, responsive God depicted in the Bible.

Just as an effect comes from a cause, a motion comes from a mover and the notion of a second derives from the notion of a first, I will suggest in the following chapters that God's meticulous involvement in time requires His timelessness, and His omnipresence in space requires His existence beyond space. Similarly, responsiveness requires a position of impassibility in order for responsiveness to be voluntary, and divine relationality requires independence in order for the relationship to be based on outgoing love rather than self-serving need. In these ways I suggest that some of what Openness has surrendered must be retained in order for its relational emphases to be worthy and valid.

In the chapters that follow I have delineated paradoxes that defend traditional notions about God, while defining them in ways to allow for the loving, relational God depicted by Openness. But I have done so in such a way as to preserve the best traditional notions which Openness in some instances has surrendered. Paradoxes covered in this volume are limited to those ideas discussed by Openness thinkers to support their conclusions. God's moral paradoxes, which may be more important—justice and mercy, grace and judgment, beneficence and punishment—are generally beyond the scope of this book.

I am using the word "paradox" in a slightly different way from its frequent use. Sometimes Christian writers use the term to refer to enigmas that must be accepted though they cannot be understood, like mysteries. I am using the word to refer to sets of concepts that initially seem to be contradictory but upon closer scrutiny will be understood as complementary. In no way am I referring to antinomies or contradictions.

This project has been undertaken with the conviction that the view I defend is both the biblical model of God and rationally consistent.

Chapter 2

Eternality and Temporality

The Old Testament says Abraham "called on the name of . . . the Everlasting God" (Genesis 21:33), which is sometimes translated "the God of eternity." In his final song of blessing Moses assured the Israelites that the "eternal God is a dwelling place" (Deuteronomy 33:27). Isaiah refers to the coming Christ as the "Eternal Father" (Isaiah 9:6), sometimes translated "the Father of eternity." Paul refers to God as "the King eternal, immortal, invisible" (1 Timothy 1:17). The writer of Hebrews speaks of "the eternal Spirit" (Hebrews 9:14).

Most theists agree that God is eternal, but they disagree about the meaning of eternality. Historically two camps have developed.

Two Views of God

The first view we will call the *timelessness* of God—the idea that God transcends time, existing on an eternal level which supersedes temporal sequence. With no past and no future, He exists eternally in the present tense.

The second view we will call the *longevity* of God—the idea that God's existence extends in both infinite regression and infinite progression, extending *ad infinitum* through both past and future, but on the level of temporal duration. Eternal means everlasting, with no beginning and no end.

In the first notion God exists above time and in the second within time. We might say that eternality in the first definition is qualitative and in the second quantitative. While the model for the second is a straight line with endless linear extension in both directions, the first is that of a circle with endless expansion, infinitely large, capable of including a straight line of endless length. Empedocles has been quoted as saying, "God is a circle whose center is everywhere and whose circumference is nowhere."[1]

Norman Geisler distinguishes between what he calls eternality and endless time.

> They are accidentally similar in that both are without end. But they are essentially different in that eternality is an essential whole, or unity; whereas time is broken up in endless parts. Both involve a "now," but the eternal now is immovable and innumerable, while the temporal now is movable and enumerable.[2]

In ancient Greece, Plato declared that God is timeless. In the fourth century A.D., Saint Augustine argued strongly for the timelessness of God, based on God's immutability, which was based on His absolute beingness. Augustine interpreted the "I AM" passage in Exodus 3:14 to refer to God's metaphysical beingness. To Augustine absolute reality, ultimate entity, infinite being, could not be subject to change. Since temporality and change are complementary, God necessarily transcends time.

In *The City of God* Augustine argues:

> If eternity and time are rightly distinguished by this, that time does not exist without some movement or

transition, while in eternity there is no change . . . there could have been no time had not some creature been made, which by some motion could give birth to change.

He adds, "Assuredly the world was made, not in time, but simultaneous with time."[3]

Thomas Aquinas wrote: "No succession occurs in God. His entire existence is simultaneous."[4] A.H. Strong argues that "God is not in time," but that "time is in God. Although there is logical succession in God's thoughts, there is no chronological succession. . . . To [God], past, present and future are 'one eternal now'."[5]

A.W. Tozer says, "God dwells in eternity but time dwells in God. He has already lived all our tomorrows as He has lived all our yesterdays. . . . For Him everything that will happen has already happened."[6] Henry C. Thiessen says God "is free from all succession of time, and he is the cause of time. . . . Eternity for God is one now, one eternal present."[7]

Paul Tillich has written a book whose title is the name Tillich used for God: *The Eternal Now*.[8] And contemporary theologian Millard J. Erickson says that "time does not apply to [God]. He was before time began."[9]

Nor is this view limited to Calvinist theologians. John Wesley himself said, "God sees and knows, from everlasting to everlasting, all that is, that was, and that is to come, through one eternal *now*. With him nothing is either past or future, but all things equally present."[10] Arminian H. Orton Wiley states: God "stands superior to time, free from temporal distinctions of past and future, and in whose life there can be no succession."[11]

Arguing against the timelessness of God, however, are such renowned names as Richard Watson and John Miley. Watson says that succession in duration is quite different from change in substance, and the two are not incompatible.[12] Miley says,

"There is no eternal now. The terms are contradictory. The notion of duration is inseparable from the notion of being, just as the notion of space is inseparable from the notion of body. Being must exist in duration."[13]

The next several pages will suggest reasons to embrace the timeless view of God rather than the longevity view.

What Time Is It?

A big problem is that we do not always know what we mean by time. We have generally thought that space is the frame for material movement, and time is the frame for occasions, occurrences and experiences. Some have put space and time together and argued that there is no such thing as time apart from spatial relationships. A day on earth is twenty-four hours, but on the moon a day is twenty-eight earth days. When we speak of days or months or years, however, we really are not speaking of time itself, but of segments of time, or divisions of time, or ways of measuring time. Certainly we often measure time by spatial position, but we also locate points in time by temporal occurrences—like "In the year of King Uzziah's death . . . " (Isaiah 6:1). We make statements like, "When I visited my relative, a certain thing happened to me."

An important question is whether occurrences are located at particular points on a temporal continuum, or whether the entire notion of time is a synthetic notion, abstracted from the relationships we observe between occurrences. Is time a "something" in which occurrences are located, or is it simply a convenient fabrication to help us understand relationships between occasions? In the mid-1980s, the Gulf War was in the world's future, but today it is in the past. The event, however, did not change. It remains constant. We have changed in relation to it. We were once before it; now we are after it. The relationship between our present experience and that occurrence is different from our relationship with it at an earlier date.

Is Time Nothing at All?

An occurrence in time may be analogous to a body in space. We think the sun sits at a certain position in space. But space is really a nothing rather than a "something." Only bodies in space are "somethings." There is no position "in space" apart from its relationship with bodies. At the same moment the sun is west to Americans, it is east to Koreans. What we call spatial positions may simply be material body relationships.

A frequent question is whether the entire universe is moving through space or standing still. One answer is that we have no way of knowing, because we can only know position in relation to another body. Since every such body exists inside the universe rather than outside, we have no outside reference point by which to recognize any movement of the universe.

Perhaps a better answer is that the universe is neither moving nor standing still, because motion and non-motion only have meaning in relation to other material objects. A fly on a car dash is sitting still in relation to the car but moving sixty miles per hour in relation to the highway. Right now I am sitting still at my desk in my study, but because of the earth's rotation I am traveling more than 1,000 miles an hour in relation to the center of the earth and even faster in orbit around the sun. Space is not an ethereal substance containing multiple locations. It is nothing, the absence of something. It contains no positions. The notion of space is purely an imaginary tool to help us understand relationships between material bodies.

Process theologian John Cobb says, "Space is understood essentially in terms of external relationships. . . . Or space is a function of . . . extension. . . . Space . . . is not to be thought of as a fixed receptacle."[14]

If this is the case and what we know as time is analogous to what we know as space, then the notion of time is simply an abstraction from occasions in the same way that space is an abstraction from material objects. Occurrences are not positioned in time any more than bodies are located in space; rather what we call time is derived from occurrences as space is derived from material bodies. Then God transcends temporal occurrences in the same way that He transcends spatial objects.

Space-Time

Another way of understanding time, however, leads to the same conclusion about God's eternality. What we have considered above may seem plausible enough until we penetrate further with more pointed questions. Just exactly what *is* the relationship between occasions and how does it differ from the relationship between bodies? Is an occurrence relationship the same as a material body relationship? If not, just what is the difference? Our only recourse is to say that one is a temporal relationship and the other is spatial. And when we have said that, we have pointed to definitions of time and space that go beyond vacuous abstractions. Here we have to define time as *duration* and space as *distance.* And on these definitions, the notion of duration is integral to occurrence and distance is integral to body, for occurrence is in a duration dimension and body is in a distance dimension. So time and space may be more than synthetic notions after all. Initially this might lead us to embrace the longevity interpretation of God's eternality, since we assume that He does experience occurrences.

At this point another provocative question screams for an answer. We know that material body belongs to the order of the material universe, but God transcends the universe and is neither measurable nor confined by distance. Does occurrence likewise belong to the created order so that God also transcends the notion of duration?

We need to note a difference between an occurrence and the experiencing of the occurrence. The first belongs to time, but the second does not necessarily do so. Though God transcends material bodies, He can still experience those bodies, and He can experience occurrences that He nevertheless transcends. Can God experience occurrences in some arrangement other than the successive order in which they occur? And if so, does it mean that He exists outside the order of duration? Could His experience, for example, be arranged in the order of concentric circles rather than in linear succession?

Twentieth-century physics has taken a strange turn in regard to space and time. Albert Einstein's special theory of relativity, dated at 1905, makes space and time interdependent. Instead of separate concepts, both were placed together as integral parts of the same concept. To the three dimensions of space— length, breadth and height—time was added as a fourth dimension, forming a four-dimensional continuum. Instead of referring to space and time as separate notions, Einstein referred to space-time.

Rather than thinking of space and time as stable fields for physical objects and occurrences, Einstein mathematically demonstrated the variability of space-time, showing how space-time is affected by material mass. Material matter with intense gravitational fields, for instance, can "layer" space around it, causing a curvature that we call a space warp.

Something similar can happen to time. When a material body is sufficiently accelerated, its dimensions decrease, distance is reduced and time slows down. Some have speculated that if an object could be accelerated to the speed of light, time for that object would stand still. And theoretically if it could be propelled faster than light, the object would go backward in time. Unfortunately this has become the substance of so much science fiction that many physicists shy away from discussing their conclusions. Nevertheless the variability of time is commonly accepted among physical scientists.

Certainly all physicists are not comfortable with the notion of going back in time, but there is more agreement on the idea of slowing time down. Conceivably then, accelerated speeds could cause time reduction in specific space fields that neighboring space fields containing less velocity would not have. A resident in an accelerated, time-reduced field could then experience an occurrence at a time prior to its occurrence in the neighboring field.

Many reputable scientists consider time travel to be theoretically possible, especially if avenues could be provided between space layers, avenues which scientists Kip Thorne (who first arrived at the notion of black holes) and Michael Morris call "wormholes."[15] If the mouth of a wormhole in one space field could be accelerated to revolve at an adequate speed, a space traveler from another field would come out the arriving mouth before he entered the first.

Because space and time are so related to matter and energy, astronomer Hugh Ross insists that space-time had a beginning.[16] This would place God above both spatial distance and temporal duration.

The purpose of this rather simplified discussion is to point out that the idea of a God who transcends time, who is able to experience in the present tense occurrences in the past or future, or who is capable of traveling back and forth in time, is not at all implausible in light of our transition from Newtonian physics to quantum physics. If God created time-space in relation to mass-energy, it would be unthinkable for us to place limitations on Him that even His creation does not necessarily have. And if time-space is a single continuum, we would not expect God to transcend space without also transcending time.

With these considerations, a tentative conclusion for the timelessness of God is difficult to resist. This conclusion will be reinforced and further explained in the next chapter, along with objections to the longevity view held by Process and Openness theologians.

Chapter 3

Timelessness and Temporal Experience

Advocates of Openness theology, agreeing with Process theism, have weighed in heavily against the timelessness of God. They insist that God is eternal in the sense of everlasting longevity, but definitely not in terms of timelessness, for several reasons.

Biblical Basis

First, they contend that the notion of divine timelessness was transported from Hellenistic philosophy and has no basis in Scripture. John Sanders[1] traces the idea from Parmenides through Plato to Philo of Alexandria and then to the Church fathers. Consequently the timelessness of God is considered foreign to pristine Christianity, a pagan attachment to the purest of Jewish-Christian tradition.

Of course, we are not interested in preserving a tradition as much as we wish to discover truth. But Openness proponents insist that the timelessness of God has no basis in Scripture. Whether they are correct is a hermeneutical matter, but even if they are correct, neither Greek advocacy nor scriptural silence on the issue implies that the notion is false. To conclude that a proposition is false because one cannot discover adequate support is called the "argument from silence" fallacy. Certain scriptural lines, however, whether interpreted correctly or not, could easily lead biblical students toward the conclusion that God is timeless, independent of Hellenistic metaphysics.

Isaiah refers to God as "the high and lofty One who inhabits eternity" (Isaiah 57:15, RSV). The idea of "inhabiting eternity" suggests a sphere of existence distinct from time, a habitat where one is not locked into temporal restrictions.

To some, Psalm 102:27 suggests more than immutability. "Thou art the same, and thy years have no end" (RSV) suggests an existence that is not segmented by temporal measurements.

Paul wrote to Timothy that Christ's grace was given to us "from all eternity" (2 Timothy 1:9), or "before the beginning of time" (NIV). To some, "from all eternity" indicates a region or zone distinct from time, and "before the beginning of time" suggests an existence outside time. If time had a beginning point and God is "from everlasting" (Psalm 90:2), then God either existed or exists outside time. The notion of "the beginning of time" could easily lead one to postulate the timelessness of God quite apart from Greek influence.

Whatever Peter meant when he said, "With the Lord one day is as a thousand years, and a thousand years as one day" (2 Peter 3:8), it should raise questions to an inquisitive mind regarding the difference between God's time system and ours.

While there is debate about the correct translation of Revelation 13:8, both the King James Version and the NIV say Christ was slain prior to the "foundation" or "creation" of the world. If Christ was not slain until near A.D. 30 yet was slain before the world, we would seem to be talking about two entirely separate systems of locating occurrences.

More than a thousand years before Christ, God met a shepherd in a remote desert and announced: "I AM WHO I AM." Then he directed, "Thus you shall say to the sons of Israel, I AM has sent me to you" (Exodus 3:14). Recent biblical students have stripped these lines of what have been thought to be ontological implications and have interpreted the verse to refer simply to God's activity. Traditionally the lines were thought to include a metaphysical connotation, referring to God's activity *based on* His eternal present-tense being. When you place this Scripture alongside Jesus' proclamation, "Before Abraham was, I am" (John 8:58, KJV, RSV), it is easy to see how Scholastic theologians thought they detected a metaphysical nuance. "Before Abraham was" (past tense), "I am" (present tense)—this suggests that Christ had existence in what to us is past, which He still refers to in the present tense.

My point here is not to give "proof-texts" for the timelessness of God, but to suggest (1) that the classical notion of God's timelessness may not have derived exclusively from Greek philosophy and (2) that the notion may in fact have some scriptural justification. William Hasker's statement that there is "no trace in the Scripture of the elaborate metaphysical and conceptual apparatus that is required to make sense of divine timelessness"[2] strikes one as irrelevant, for such a claim is not generally made by those who embrace the view.

Incomprehensible Timelessness

A second objection raised by Openness to the timelessness of God has to do with our difficulty in comprehending such a notion. Clark Pinnock states, "It is hard to form any idea of what timelessness might mean, since all of our thinking is temporally conditioned."[3] Hasker says, A "main difficulty about divine timelessness is that it is very hard to make clear logical sense of the doctrine."[4]

Certainly no one can say that timelessness is easy to understand. Theologians have never made that claim, nor have they intimated that anyone could ever comprehend the notion, even with great difficulty. Albeit, Hasker himself admits that

25

the logical difficulties with the notion of timelessness are probably solvable.[5]

But conceding the notion is difficult is precisely the same admission we make about many other doctrines of God that we embrace with great conviction. The idea of divine immensity is beyond our understanding. Believing in divine omnipotence is intellectually humiliating because one cannot arrive at the notion by rational analysis. Infiniteness itself, in any area, defies human comprehension.

Tozer said, "To admit that there is One who . . . exists outside our categories . . . who will not appear before the bar of our reason . . . requires a great deal of humility. . . . We save face by thinking God down to our level, or at least down to where we can manage Him."[6] A psalm quotes God as saying, "You thought I was altogether like you" (Psalm 50:21, NIV). Through Isaiah God said, "For My thoughts are not your thoughts, neither are your ways My ways. . . . For as the heavens are higher than the earth, so are My ways higher than your ways, and My thoughts than your thoughts" (55:8-9).

Beliefs should require evidence, but they do not have to require understanding in order to be credible. Even natural science accepts hypotheses as factual based on experimentation alone, and it uses such words as "instinct" and "phenomenon" to cover items of belief based on supporting evidence which cannot be understood. Paul spoke of knowing that which "surpasses knowledge" and experiencing what is "beyond all that we ask or think" (Ephesians 3:19-20).

For me, one of the most difficult beliefs to understand is the longevity of God, which Openness strongly supports. No way can I conceive of an existence through an eternal past. My imagination stretches to its limits, and I do not even approach an understanding of a God who never had a beginning. To abandon belief in the timelessness of God because it cannot be understood would require me to trash belief in the other view of eternality as well—unless I have other reasons to accept longevity that I do not have for timelessness. Indeed, I can come nearer to understanding in the timeless model how God never had a beginning than I can in linear longevity. But even then it is beyond my comprehension.

Objections to timelessness based on incomprehensibility would rule out not only the longevity of God but belief in God Himself, a belief for which we nevertheless have adequate rationale.

God's Temporality

A third, perhaps primary, reason proponents of Openness reject the timelessness of God is based on the assumption that divine timelessness would imply God could not be involved on the temporal level of succession and interact with occurrences sequentially as they occur. To them, timelessness implies something like a distant deistic God who is cut off from developing situations in the world and in the lives of human beings. This would preclude the basic proposition of Openness theology, that God is dynamic in the world rather than passive, solicitously involved in human dilemmas, responding efficaciously to human petition, reacting to human sin.

Assuming that a timeless God could not be involved in time, advocates of Openness oppose divine timelessness in principle. Pinnock writes, "Timelessness limits God. If he were timeless, God would be unable to work salvation in history, would be cut off from the world, have no real relationship with people and would be completely static."[7] Hasker asks, "If God is truly timeless . . . how can God act in time? How can he know what is occurring on the changing earthly scene?"[8]

The primary thesis of Openness theology is that God is dynamic rather than static, active in the world rather than passive, involved rather than aloof. This emphasis causes those of us to rejoice who wholeheartedly concur.

What some of us cannot understand, however, is how this conclusion requires the premise that God is not timeless. Openness admits that God can be infinite without preventing His involvement with the finite, He can be transcendent without preventing immanence, He can be omnipotent while being voluntarily vulnerable, He can be beyond space without preventing His presence in space. Being divine did not even prevent His becoming human while remaining divine in the incarnation. Why can God not be timeless without it inhibiting His involvement in time? To ask it another way, why can He not be active in time without being confined to time?

Pinnock himself even suggests, "God creates a non-divine world" as "an echo in space and time of the communion that God experiences in eternity."[9] He seems to be saying that God creates in time and space an echo of His experience outside of time and space. Pinnock even suggests that God is "transcendent to temporal passage" and "transcends our experience of time,"[10] but then he mitigates the meaning of those phrases by explaining that God is simply immune to the negative effects of time.

My point is that God is capable of experiencing time without being caged in time. He can be involved in successive occurrences in time without being limited by time. He can function in temporality while belonging to a timeless eternity. God does not have to exist in time in order to experience time.

And my further point is that God can interact with the occurrences of time from a position of timelessness more completely than He could do if He were confined to time. A Creator can be more microscopically and exhaustively involved in His creation than a creature can be. Only an infinite God can be minutely and thoroughly involved in the finite. To sacrifice the timelessness of God is to curtail His ability to function on the level of time in meticulous detail. A timeless God can participate in all occurrences of time more attentively than a temporal God could possibly do.

One reason to accept the timelessness of God comes from the evidence we have for God's foreknowledge. Rather than excluding Him from the processes of the world, timelessness allows God to be involved without sacrificing foreknowledge, in a way that will be explained in a later chapter. A God who is free from time is in a position to experience past, present and future occurrences simultaneously and to weave them into a pattern or orchestrate them into a symphony.

Eternal God in a Temporal World

It remains to be asked in what precise way God is timeless and on what model or analogy can we come nearer understanding it. How can God function in time while remaining in a timeless dimension?

It has often been illustrated by the picture of a person watching a parade from a high-rise apartment or a high tower, as Thomas Aquinas pictured it, capable of seeing every part of the parade at once. This analogy is helpful, but it breaks down in not eliminating time sequence in the person who watches. Another illustration is that of watching a delayed telecast, videotaped earlier. The ball game or the news footage occurs to the one who watches it after it occurred to the ones who taped it. This is more like what happens when God experiences a temporal occurrence outside the time frame in which it occurred.

Distinction needs to be made between two areas of God's experience. He experiences His temporal creation, which includes the material universe as well as conscious beings, presumably including the angelic order—and any other order of creation that we may not be aware of. But there is a larger area of God's experience about which we know very little, the area of His own eternal order quite apart from His creation. A transcendent God occupies a realm beyond the world, and His experience within Himself does not require relationship with the world. Surely His Trinitarian relationships are intensely intimate, of which the closest human relationship is only a faint facsimile.

When we assert the timelessness of God, we refer first to His experience in His own realm of eternity. Second, by His timelessness we mean the God in eternity is in a position to experience every occurrence in the world simultaneously at any time that He might wish, prior to or after its occurrence in time. Since His creation is ordered on an arrangement of successive duration, however, God in relation to the world also experiences the occurrences of the world successively, as they occur. Both eternal occurrence and successive occurrence are equally accessible to God.

Furthermore, experiencing occurrences both eternally and successively is not contradictory. My children watch old movies over and over and re-experience the occurrences in the movies each time they watch. Just as God can locate every object in space, He can locate every occurrence in time, and just as He can access all objects to Himself, He can access all occurrences at once. He is confined neither by space nor time. He fills both space and time with Himself and embraces both space and time in His eternality. He is as independent of duration as He is of locality, yet can function in time as easily as in space.

Isaiah said, "Thus says the high and lofty One who inhabits eternity, whose name is Holy: 'I dwell in the high and holy place. . . .'" After so magnificent a declaration, God immediately adds, "[I dwell] also with him who is of a contrite and humble spirit" (Isaiah 57:15, RSV).

Richard Rice argues against timelessness by saying, "[God] decides before he acts, he acts after he decides. This is so simple that it sounds trivial."[11] This argument overlooks the fact that God's decisions and actions may be in separate areas, the first in the eternal dimension and the second in the temporal. Rice's point would be pertinent only if we have prior knowledge that both the decisions and actions were on the temporal level. Assuming one's conclusion in the premise is called begging the question.

In a restricted sense we humans also have a measure of independence or detachment from time, in that we as persons experience self-identity, or continuity of individuality, through time. Our experience of occurrences changes, but our experience of selfhood remains constant. This kind of independence from temporal occurrences may be necessary for recognizing variable experiences as successive. Though we recognize them as successive as they occur, we often relive past occasions and anticipate future occurrences, experiencing both past and future in the present.

Two Pictures

Here I wish to suggest optional paradigms to help explain the timelessness of God, both of which at best are flimsy similes. The first is a straight line to represent the linear forward movement of time. On this line is placed every occurrence at a point in temporal relation to other occurrences, a relation that we call succession. The line has a beginning but has no end. Immortal humans and angels extend forward endlessly in everlasting duration. On this line God can move back and forth to experience occasions that are in the past or future, as He pleases. Or He can occupy all positions at once, experiencing all past and future occurrences at the same time. One way to say it is that all the past and future are present with God. Another way is to say that God is forever present in all the past and future. Either way, succession of thoughts and experiences is not necessary to divine consciousness.

Human beings have mechanisms for imitating timelessness through memory and anticipation, experiencing both past and future in the present. But these mechanisms at best are only substitutes and imitations of divine timelessness.

Why then can God not undo the past or redo it? If He walks back into the past, why can He not change it? The answer is that when we speak of past occurrences, we are speaking of events that occurred in time. While God is not confined to time, those occurrences are, and logically they cannot be changed. A happening cannot un-happen. A moment once lived cannot become un-lived. An act committed cannot become uncommitted. Locked into temporal sequence, the events cannot be timeless.

The second paradigm, with all its limitations, represents the eternality of God. It is a picture of concentric spheres in infinite expanse, filling in eternity whatever is analogous to both space and time. Within this schema, God's experience takes the form of a more all-encompassing spherical pattern than linear duration. His experience is arranged in many and various orders, one of which may be temporal or chronological. Another arrangement is based on genre, with various suborders based on different kinds of experience. Another order is based on the different personalities with whom He relates, another on the kinds of feeling that are inherent in the experiences. There may be many other arrangements based on ingredients of which we have no idea.

God is capable of accessing any order of experiences or every experience in every arrangement at once, as He may wish. An eternity without bounds is embraced by a God without limit, encircling and enveloping all occurrences, filling all eternity with Himself and holding all eternity within Himself! While it may be appropriate to say that God "endure[s]" (Psalm 102:26), the notion of duration is meaningless when applied to God's *experience*. If His past and future experience is not limited to past and future, then God exists experientially in the eternal now.

This is not to say that God makes no distinctions between occurrences in time or experiences in eternity, but that all

32

experiences are equally present to Him, not obscured by temporal duration. Nor have I said that temporal sequence is excluded from God's experience, but on His eternal level it *can* be excluded. And God may even temporarily block off His eternal experience of future occurrences in the world in order to activate His spontaneous response. If so, it is voluntary on His part rather than essential to what He is.

Chapter 4

Foreknowledge and Contingency

C hristian theism makes an astounding claim that God is perfect in knowledge, based on Scriptures too numerous to delineate here. The notion of divine omniscience—"omni-science," all-knowing—is also deduced from the conviction that God is infinite.

Some, however, think they have detected logical contradictions in the doctrine and have modified the meaning of the term to mitigate the problem. Process theology has avoided the problem by redefining God Himself as finite and consequently denying the idea of omniscience altogether.

Among traditional theists, what is open to debate is just how much knowledge is meant by "all-knowing," especially in regard to the future. The Bible speaks in several places of God's "foreknowledge" (Romans 8:29, 11:2; 1 Peter 1:2), sometimes called prescience, of future events. In Isaiah God suggests that His authentic deity can be recognized by His ability to forecast accurately the future. Caustically He said, "Present your case. . . . Declare to us what is going to take place . . . Announce to us what is coming. Declare the things that are going to come afterward, That we may know that you are gods" (41:21-23).

Problems arise in seeking to ascertain how much of the future God knows and in what way(s) He knows it. Does He have knowledge of future occurrences that are still open options, yet to be determined by beings who have the free power to determine? If so, does God's advance knowledge of what will occur determine the choices those beings will make? If choices are free, people should be able to cause an occurrence different from what God foreknew, which would mean His foreknowledge was false. But if God's foreknowledge does determine their choices, it would mean their choices are not free. Yet if God does not have advance knowledge of the choices each person will make, can we really say that He is omniscient, knowing everything?

Determinism

To analyze the problem and seek a solution, we need to understand three kinds of foreknowledge, or three ways that God may foreknow, the last of which will be the most controversial.

The first is *determinism*. In philosophy this term generally refers to mechanical determination by natural or psychological causes, a view that is pushed by naturalistic materialism to preclude any human freedom. In theology we use it to refer to God's determination of what He intends to cause. I can foreknow that my lawn will be mowed by evening because I intend to do it. I can accurately predict that my long-range project will be completed because I purpose to see it through. God can predict any occurrence that He determines to cause.

The psalmist seems to say that God foreknew his life because God intended it and knew that He would follow through on His intentions: "And in Thy book they were all written, the days that were ordained for me, when as yet there was not one of them" (Psalm 139:16). In Isaiah God is quoted as saying, "Surely, just as I have intended so it has happened, and just as

I have planned so it will stand" (14:24). Again God said, "From ancient times I planned it. Now I have brought it to pass" (37:26). Again God said,

> I am God, and there is no one like Me,
> Declaring the end from the beginning
> And from ancient times things
>   which have not been done,
> Saying, "My purpose will be established,
> And I will accomplish all my good pleasure." . . .
> Truly I have spoken; truly I will bring it to pass.
> I have planned it, surely I will do it. (46:9-11)

In Jeremiah God declared the good things He intends to do for His people, and nine times in one short passage God said, "I will" (32:37-41)! A Hebrew psalm says, "The plans of the LORD stand firm forever, the purposes of his heart through all generations" (33:11, NIV).

In the New Testament Paul writes that God "chose us . . . before the foundation of the world, that we should be holy" (Ephesians 1:4), that He "called us . . . according to his own purpose . . . from all eternity" (2 Timothy 1:9), and that we have "the hope of eternal life, which God, who cannot lie, promised long ages ago" (Titus 1:2).

Most theists agree that God foreknows whatever in the future He intends to accomplish, to cause or to do. His foreknowledge is based on His determination. At this point, however, differences of opinion arise in two areas. The first has to do with how much God determines and how much He allows free human choices to determine—and how much He allows to be determined by natural causes.

Some claim John Calvin held that God knows all the future in minute detail simply because God determines every future occurrence—that nothing has ever occurred nor ever will occur that God has not specifically decreed. They hold that God, being meticulously sovereign, decreed the "fall of man" (sometimes called supralapsarianism), and He chooses and calls whom He wishes to be saved (called predestination), determining the moral choices for salvation they will make. Most Christians agree that God could know all the future if He should determine every occurrence, but they question whether God chooses to be so precisely deterministic, usurping all human freedom.

Certainly some Scriptures depict God's prescience of future events without specifically indicating that He will determine them. "Behold, the former things have come to pass, now I declare new things; before they spring forth I proclaim them to you" (Isaiah 42:9). "And who is like Me? Let him proclaim and declare it. . . . let them declare . . . the things that are coming and the events that are going to take place. . . . Have I not long since announced it to you and declared it?" (44:7-8).

Assuming God does not determine every future detail, Christian scholars have a second difference of opinion regarding whether God knows future items that He will not determine—that is, whether He has any foreknowledge based on anything other than determinism. Does He know contingencies, occurrences that are dependent either on future free human choices or future natural causes, occurrences that he chooses not to determine? The old Socinians denied that God had any foreknowledge of contingent events, but most Christians throughout Church history have believed that God has foreknowledge of occurrences beyond those that He determines.

Causality

A second possible kind of foreknowledge, or a second way that God may foreknow, is what we will call *causality*. In philosophy the term is often used synonymously with material determinism, but here I am using it to refer to advance knowledge one can have of any occurrence that is expected to be an effect of a cause that one already knows. We are aware of cause-and-effect relationships, and we can accurately predict certain effects from knowing certain causes.

This applies to psychological causes as well as natural causes. People often behave in predictable ways based on motives, incentives, drives, desires, circumstances. While they may still have freedom to act otherwise, they often can be expected to behave in ways that are caused by certain overwhelming influences. That they *can* act otherwise does not mean that they *will*. If we know the conditions that direct their choices, we can often anticipate the choices they will make. And our correct expectation of their choices does not in any way determine what their choices will be. If only two entrees are on a restaurant menu, liver and shrimp, I can be sure in advance what my wife will order, but my advance knowledge does not determine her choice.

Many effects become causes to produce future effects, which become causes for further effects, which in turn become causes for more effects. Causal chains, both natural and human, continue indefinitely, like the domino theory. Many occurrences are direct effects of immediate causes and also indirect effects from remote causes. Several causal chains often converge at the same time and place, producing effects that would be different if one of the causes were missing. Most occurrences are effects of more than one cause, both immediate and remote. The process is intricately complex. Myriad causes are operative in the world, capable of multiple combinations for innumerable effects in a mind-boggling complication that would grind the most sophisticated computer to a nervous breakdown. Yet if there is no divine or human interference with causality, the effects are mechanically calculable if all causes could be known and programmed in precise proportion.

Divine omniscience is "programmed" with an exhaustive

assortment of every single cause and every multiple causal combination, constantly producing on the readout a complex conglomerate of meticulous effects. Based on His comprehensive knowledge of every present cause, God can know future effects purely on the principle of causality.

Direct Knowledge

Those who hold that every trivial occurrence is specifically determined by God's decrees do not need to resort to causality to postulate perfect foreknowledge. Those who hold that each occurrence is either determined by God or effected by prior causality can posit God's omniscient foreknowledge on a combination of determinism and causality.

Many Christians agree that some events are determined by God and some by natural causes, and that God is in a position to know both kinds of occurrences in advance. The preponderant opinion of a large body of Christians, however, is that some events are neither predetermined by God nor effected by mechanical causation. The ability of human beings to determine some occurrences by free autonomy will be discussed in a later chapter. Assuming that people are free to determine some future events that cannot be accurately predicted by causality, however, forces us to conclude either that God does not know that portion of the future that is contingent on human free choice, or that He has a third way of foreknowing, or a third kind of foreknowledge.

This third kind of foreknowledge we will call *direct knowledge*. If we use the label "direct vision" as some have done, we must remember that "vision" is used as a metaphor that calls to mind the idea of photons, eyeball retinas and optic nerves, items that are inappropriate to God. The first two kinds of knowledge, determinism and causality, are indirect knowledge. God knows future events indirectly, through His will to determine or through causes with which He is acquainted. But many would claim that future events are present with God in such a way that He knows them directly—with "immediate" rather than "mediate" knowledge, with a knowledge that is direct rather than mediated to Him through other items.

Some Arminians have believed in what has been called middle knowledge, that God not only knows all *actual* events but also all *possible* events from all possible natural or human contingencies. Traditional Calvinists have rejected the idea because they have rejected all contingencies. It would seem that if God knows all possible options that persons with free choice might choose, He could compute those possible choices into the causality complex and know their long-range "ripple effects." This kind of middle knowledge, however, would not be based on direct knowledge but on causality. Openness proponents have insisted that it would be logically impossible for God to have direct knowledge of non-events—to know a nothing—in the same way that it is impossible for God to draw a square circle or create an uncreated world. To subscribe to the notion of God's direct knowledge of future events, however, does not require God to have middle knowledge of future non-events.

Human Freedom

While strongly embracing human freedom, Openness theology denies God's direct knowledge of any future event. This combination of beliefs leads Openness advocates to modify the traditional understanding of omniscience by postulating a foreknowledge that is less than absolute. Pinnock writes: "If choices are real and freedom significant, future decisions cannot be exhaustively foreknown. . . . God knows everything that can be known—but God's foreknowledge does not include the undecided. . . . God is all-knowing in the sense that he knows all that is possible to know."[1] Hasker argues, "It is logically impossible that God should have foreknowledge of a genuinely free action."[2] David Basinger says, "God can never know with certainty what will happen in any context involving freedom of choice."[3]

Some of us are convinced, to the contrary, that Scripture strongly leads us to believe that God foreknew future free choices in a way that cannot be adequately explained by either determinism or causality. If God did foreknow human action in a way that was more than an educated guess and did not violate human freedom, then foreknowledge must have been direct knowledge of that future action.

The Suffering Servant passage (Isaiah 53) describes human reaction to Christ some seven hundred years in advance.

> He was despised and forsaken of men, . . .
> And like one from whom men hide their face,
> He was despised, and we did not esteem Him. . . .
> Yet we ourselves esteemed Him stricken,
> Smitten of God, and afflicted.
> But He was pierced through. . . .
> He was crushed . . . ;
> The chastening . . . fell upon Him,
> And . . . scourging. . . .
> He was oppressed and He was afflicted . . .
> Like a lamb that is led to slaughter. . . .
> By oppression and judgment He was taken away;
> . . . His generation . . . considered
> That He was cut off out of the land of the living. . . .
> His grave was assigned to be with wicked men. . . ."
>
> (53:3-9)

This description of human reaction is rather specific, given centuries before it occurred. It is obviously more than an educated guess based on multiple causality. Either all those involved in the conspiracy were robots with no freedom, allowing God to foreknow by determinism, or God had direct foreknowledge of their actions and reactions.

Through Isaiah God said, "Before they call, I will answer" (65:24). Here God is probably referring either to the millennium or to a restored earth, but whatever the period or situation, the principle remains. If God answers before the request, He knows what the request will be. Unless those who make the request are automatons, locked up in a deterministic, causal system, God has direct knowledge in advance of what they will freely request.

Throughout the Bible, the basic assumption of trustworthy prophecy was divine foreknowledge, yet the fulfillment of much of the prophecy required free human volition. If the predicted actions of those involved were too distant from present causes and too subtle or complex to predict by causality, advance knowledge of those actions had to be direct. Daniel said to Nebuchadnezzar, "[T]here is a God in heaven who reveals mysteries, and He has made known . . . what will take place in the latter days" (Daniel 2:28).

All three synoptic Gospels record Peter's thrice denial of Christ (cf. Mark 14:30, 66-72). Earlier in the day, against Peter's protest, Jesus told him he would deny three times before the cock crowed twice. The foretold specifics in this episode, most of which involve free choice, defy explanation on the principle of causality. Of the twelve disciples, one of them was approached by three separate individuals identifying him with Christ's followers. Three times he denied it. The cock crowed the second time after the third denial. To account for Christ's advance knowledge of this extraordinary combination of occurrences by pointing to causal motives, incentives and circumstances is perfectly implausible. Christ foreknew some things that could only be foreknown by direct knowledge.

Earlier I alluded to "the Lamb that was slain from the creation of the world" (Revelation 13:8, NIV). This implies that God knew in advance the human race would fall into sin. If "the deck was stacked" so heavily in favor of Adam's fall that God foreknew it by causality, God can be indicted as a party to the fall for positioning humankind in such a vulnerable position to begin with. And that would discredit God's justice. But if God allowed Adam enough freedom to make him responsible, then the fall was not a foregone certainty and it could only be foreknown by direct knowledge. The alternate reading of the verse leads to the same conclusion.

Enter Eternality

In spite of overwhelming scriptural evidence, proponents of Openness argue against direct foreknowledge of contingent events. They admit God's direct knowledge of past and present occurrences and God's foreknowledge of those future events that can be known by determinism or predicted by causality. But to them, knowing future contingent events that are yet undecided by those who have the freedom to decide those events is logically contradictory.

On the surface the argument seems consistent and the conclusions valid. Closer observation, however, reveals that the logic makes sense only on their prior rejection of the timelessness of God.

Certain theologians like Richard Watson[4] and John Miley[5] have argued strongly for God's direct foreknowledge while denying His timelessness. If timelessness is rejected, it seems more consistent to reject direct knowledge also, as Openness has done. But if my earlier argument for divine timelessness is correct, God's direct knowledge of future contingencies should be expected. The Scripture is consistent, supporting both propositions.

What we on our level call foreknowledge is in fact present knowledge to a timeless, eternal God. The scriptural term, like most biblical language, accommodates our thought categories to facilitate understanding of truth that cannot be verbally communicated with precision. John Wesley wrote:

"With [God] nothing is past or future, but all things equally present. He has, therefore . . . no foreknowledge, no afterknowledge. . . . Yet when he speaks to us . . . he lets himself down to our capacity. . . . In condescension to our weakness, he speaks of his own . . . foreknowledge."[6]

Failing to distinguish between the object of knowledge and the subject of knowledge—or between what God knows and the knowing itself—will lead one to think that direct knowledge of future contingent events is contradictory. But the direct knowledge is *knowing* and the future event is *what God knows*. The knowledge is on God's level and is timeless. The event that He knows is on our level and is past, present or future. What God knows can be temporal while the knowledge itself is timeless. A.H. Strong says, "Time is a form of finite thought to which the divine mind is not subject."[7] If God is in fact timeless, then His eternal knowledge of temporal occurrences is not only possible but very probable.

Clark Pinnock suggests we should ask ourselves whether "God *could* create a world . . . where he would not foreknow all decisions of his creatures in advance." Then he answers, "Surely this must be possible if God is all-powerful."[8] Even if God could do so, that alone would not mean that He did. Pinnock would agree. But I am not at all convinced that God could make such a world in the first place. God's omniscience is analogous to His omnipotence, and God cannot limit His knowledge any more than He can limit His power. It would be like saying God could create a stone too big for Himself to lift. Because both omnipotence and omniscience are intrinsic to God, neither can be limited. Certainly God can refuse to function from either of them, but that is something quite different. Though God can limit His *use* of either knowledge or power, He cannot limit either of them and remain God. How He can refuse to *function* from them will be clarified in the next two chapters.

The Freedom Dilemma

Defending God's direct foreknowledge of contingent events raises another problem that I alluded to in the beginning of the chapter, a problem that has been clearly articulated by many dissenters. If God knows in advance what I will freely choose, how can I be free to choose otherwise? Does not perfect foreknowledge amount to determinism, preempting any measure of freedom for anybody?

In *Paradise Lost*, John Milton questions whether God has perfect foreknowledge, but if He does, Milton emphatically states it does not determine a person's choices. In these lines, God is talking:

> They, therefore, as to right belonged,
> So were created, nor can justly accuse
> Their Maker, or their making, or their fate,
> As if predestination overruled
> Their will, disposed by absolute decree
> Or high foreknowledge. They themselves
>   decreed
> Their own revolt, not I. If I foreknew,
> Foreknowledge had no influence on their
>   fault. . . .
> So without least impulse or shadow of fate,
> Or aught by me immutably foreseen,
> They trespass. . . . [9]

John Calvin avoided the problem by denying human freedom to make any choice that God did not decree. Jacobus Arminius held that God's advance knowledge was determined by what the person would freely choose in the future, rather than the choice being determined by God's advance knowledge. Process theology averts the problem by sacrificing God's absolute foreknowledge of contingent events. Similarly, Openness, which strongly emphasizes human free choice, solves the problem by denying God's direct foreknowledge of events that are contingent on free choice. Pinnock says, "Exhaustive foreknowledge . . . would imply a fixity of events."[10] Hasker says, "There are serious questions concerning the logical compatibility of comprehensive divine foreknowledge and libertarian free will. . . . [Comprehensive foreknowledge] means that the future event God knows is already fixed and unalterable . . . so one does not have free choice."[11]

There are two problems, however, with this conclusion. First, it confuses the notion of knowledge with influence, and makes knowledge deterministic. But knowledge by definition is not causal or determinative. Freedom is opposite coercion; it is not opposite knowledge or certainty. The proposition, "It will not happen otherwise," can be deduced from knowledge, but "It cannot happen otherwise" would be a false inference.

If I should offer my daughter the option of owning a kitten or a puppy, I know in advance she would choose the kitten, but her choice is not caused by my advance knowledge. This is not a perfect analogy because my foreknowledge of her choice is based on causality rather than direct knowledge—I know her likes and dislikes that would strongly influence her choice. But the illustration serves to point out that advance knowledge, whatever the basis, is not determinative. Thiessen says, "The knowledge of the future is not itself causative. Free actions do not take place because they are foreseen, but they are foreseen because they will take place."[12]

A second problem with the Openness conclusion is that it is based on what I have argued is a false premise—that God is confined to time. Hasker gives a four-point deduction based on three premises[13] to prove it is logically impossible for God to have foreknowledge of a genuinely free action. The premises as well as the deductions, however, are drawn on the unstated assumption that God is locked into time sequence. If God is timeless, as much of historic Christendom has held and the Scriptures strongly hint, then what God eternally knows about me will not inhibit my freedom to act in what to me is future.

This suggests an epistemological distinction that is generally known but often overlooked—a distinction between propositional knowledge on the one hand, by which we mean knowledge of fact or truth, and personal knowledge on the other, by which we mean acquaintance or familiarity. The first is knowledge *that* and the second is knowledge *of*. It is the difference between "I know that you are a good person" and "I know you," or between "I know that my Redeemer lives" and "I know my Redeemer." Much of our propositional knowledge comes from our personal knowledge—I can know *that* you exist because I know *you*, or I know that an event occurred because I am acquainted with the event.

Those who subscribe to the timelessness of God hold that God knows what events will occur in a person's future because in His timelessness He knows those events. He is familiar with them; He is acquainted with them. He knows that the events will occur because He knows the events themselves. What we have not yet chosen is eternally present with Him. This is what we call direct knowledge. God's knowledge *that* certain events will occur on one level is based on His direct knowledge of those events on another.

If what we call God's advance knowledge were actual *fore*-knowledge, it would be on the level of time. But to God it is not foreknowledge. It is eternal timeless knowledge, *determined by* temporal choices rather than *determining* those choices. Because God's knowledge is in a timeless dimension, it need not affect occurrences in a temporal dimension.

Chapter 5

Omniscience and Non-consciousness

A dvocates of Openness insist that perfect foreknowledge edge would make God incapable of responding to future events with surprise, delight or dismay. It would make God's interaction with human experiences formal rather than genuine, and would preempt any responsive spontaneity on God's part. Clark Pinnock says, "God . . . responds and adapts to surprises and to the unexpected. . . . If Plan A fails, God is ready with Plan B."[1] Again he says, "God . . . is still learning what the world is becoming."[2]

Earlier I proposed that God's genuine involvement in the world can be retained without sacrificing His foreknowledge by recognizing the timelessness of God. In this chapter I am suggesting a distinction that will make perfect foreknowledge and openness compatible concepts even if God were not timeless. And I insist that this move is philosophically, psychologically and scripturally sound.

A Real Distinction

While the difference between *knowledge* and *consciousness* is a fine distinction, it is so obvious that we wonder how we could have overlooked it for so long. Even one of my undergraduate students argued that he deserved an "A" instead of a failing grade because he knew all the answers that he just could not think of. People know a million times more than they are conscious of at any moment. God seemed to be referring to His conscious awareness rather than His specific knowledge when He said, "Nor had it entered My mind that they should do this abomination, to cause Judah to sin" (Jeremiah 32:35).

Certainly we must maintain that God's consciousness is big enough to embrace everything at once if He should so choose. But "knowledge of" and "consciousness of" are categorically distinct, and the second does not follow necessarily from the first. Omniscience refers to perfect knowledge rather than consciousness. Whether God is every minute conscious of everything is another matter, but the claim is not entailed in the proposition of omniscience.

Shades of this epistemological distinction were foreshadowed by the seventeenth-century controversy between British empiricism and continental rationalism. John Locke defined mind as consciousness, insisting that nothing qualified to be called mind outside of consciousness. Leibnitz retorted that Locke admits memory is in the mind without being in consciousness, which Leibnitz thought made the noted empiricist in reality a closet rationalist.[3]

While the Scripture in some places leads us to believe God knows everything, several lines refer to God's forgetting or not remembering (Psalm 88:5; Isaiah 43:25; Jeremiah 23:39; 31:34; Hebrews 8:12). Though these lines may simply refer to the way God chooses to deal with certain people or situations, if they do refer literally to forgetting and not remembering they would seem to contradict omniscience. If God forgets anything, how can He know everything? If God should both remember and forget the same item in the same way at the same time, it would be a logical contradiction. But if omniscience refers to knowledge and forgetting refers to consciousness, we have no contradiction.

Some 200 years ago Adam Clarke suggested God might choose to know only what He wishes to know, which Clarke thought would not violate the notion of omniscience because whatever ignorance God has would be voluntary.[4] Other divines suggested that all contingencies are finite and God could choose not to know finite contingencies. Those views, however, leave God less than omniscient, because omniscience means that God does in fact have all knowledge, not that He is selective in knowledge. Those who use the analogy of omnipotence, saying that God can refuse to know something without affecting His omniscience just as He can refuse to function from power without affecting His omnipotence, are comparing apples with oranges. It is a weak analogy because refusing to use His power does not reduce God's power, but a refusal to know some things does reduce God's knowledge.

What I am suggesting is that God may choose to block out of conscious awareness certain items that He does not wish to contemplate, items that He nevertheless knows. God has perfect mental control. He can refuse to think of whatever He does not wish His mind to rest on. His ability to do so is included in His omnipotence. But because it is a self-limitation of consciousness rather than knowledge, God's omniscience is not impugned. Even all future contingencies remain instantly accessible to God.

Certainly God is not slipshod or haphazard in what He blocks out of consciousness. His thinking is perfectly disciplined. Nothing slides out without being intentionally expelled. Nor is God's ability to forget without moral restraint. Nothing drifts out that should be retained. What He keeps in consciousness and what He keeps out are consistent with His moral nature. Over and again the Scripture says that God "remembers" His covenant (Genesis 9:15; Exodus 2:24; Psalm 105:8; Ezekiel 16:60).

Asserting the distinction between knowledge and conscious-ness may be thoughtlessly disparaged as a pedantic exercise in triviality. Some may think it is a distinction without a differ-ence. But I insist that God's ability to control His thoughts is neither trifling nor impertinent. When we observe the same ability in human beings, we consider it a meritorious virtue. God's personal mind-control is not a game of pretense to manipulate Himself, but a prudent exercise to facilitate His relationship with the world. The following paragraphs will suggest areas where it may be operative.

Past Sins and Future Lostness

First is the area of God's forgiveness of human sin. God said, "I, even I, am the one who wipes out your transgressions for My own sake; and I will not remember your sins" (Isaiah 43:25). Again God declared, "I will forgive their iniquity, and their sin I will remember no more" (Jeremiah 31:34; see also Hebrews 8:12).

Openness proponents insist that God knows everything it is possible to know, and certainly it is possible for God to know past human sins. But here God declares He will not remember those sins that are forgiven. If God's not remembering, how-ever, refers to consciousness rather than knowledge, God has a way to "forget" human sin without affecting His omniscience. God's ability to block items out of consciousness can apply to the past as well as the future. While God's perfect knowledge will forever include our sins, as far as conscious awareness is concerned they have been buried in the sea of His forgetful-ness.

The second area regards future lostness. Someone may say, "If God knows in advance that I will be ultimately lost, surely His attempts to bring me to repentance and commitment are insincere since He knows the attempts are futile. Toying with me is insulting."

While the New Testament specifically says God foreknows those who will respond to His call (Romans 8:29; 11:2), it does not say He foreknows those who will reject. Though their rejection may be in His knowledge bank, God may on occasion refuse to "call up" such pieces of knowledge to active consciousness, like a computer operator refusing to bring up to the screen what is on the hard drive. He may wish to function consciously from uncertainty about their future, so as not to undermine His sincere motive to bring them into the kingdom. God's ability to keep contingencies out of mind enables Him to watch a person, like looking over the shoulder of a chess player, encouraging him, motivating him and hoping he will make the right moves. Operating on the level of time, He shuts off from conscious awareness a measure of His timeless knowledge.

Predictive Prophecies

A third area of operation for God's non-consciousness has to do with predictive prophecies that are contingent on human behavior. Some prophecies are based on God's determination to do what He has declared; they are irrevocable, and their fulfillment is certain. Other prophecies were given within certain sets of circumstances and were understood to be conditioned by those circumstances. They were not considered false prophecies if they were given with the understanding that they could be repealed if the circumstances changed. Such was the case with many predictions whose fulfillment was contingent on the moral behavior of the people.

God instructed Jonah to proclaim that within forty days "Nineveh will be overthrown" (Jonah 3:4). Though God as usual did not enunciate all His modifications and disclaimers, the king understood that it was a contingent prophecy. So he instructed the people to repent, and said, "Who knows, God may turn and relent, and withdraw His burning anger so that we shall not perish?" (3:9). And what happened? "When God saw their deeds, that they turned from their wicked way, then God relented concerning the calamity which He had declared He would bring upon them. And He did not do it" (3:10).

Richard Rice objects, "If God knows the future exhaustively, then conditional prophecies lose their integrity. They do not express a genuine divine intention. They are nothing more than hypothetical assertions that God fully knows will never be realized."[5]

Rice's point is credible on the assumption that perfect advance knowledge is tantamount to full consciousness of all contingencies. If God, however, refused to access to immediate awareness what He nevertheless knew so that He could react temporally and successively to the moral state of the Ninevites, then the prophecy does not lose its integrity. It was a genuine divine intention under the given circumstances, and it was not a hypothetical assertion.

In connection with the Jonah episode Pinnock says, "God experiences temporal passage, learns new facts when they occur and changes plans in response to what humans do."[6] If we can interpret "learning new facts" to mean "acquisitioning otherwise known facts" or "becoming aware of what He otherwise knows" rather than "acquiring new knowledge," then the line communicates important truth about God. If God, while functioning in time, should choose to shut out of consciousness certain timeless knowledge, then He would experience temporal passage, He would "become aware" of new facts as they occur and He could change plans in response to what humans do. But that does not require God to be ignorant of the future, only that He is not functioning consciously from that knowledge.

Human Petition and Divine Purposes

A fourth area has to do with God's response to human petition. God may respond to some prayers, having previously kept out of consciousness that the specific prayers would be made. Being consciously unaware of future petitions is different from not knowing what those petitions will be. The first does not preclude the possibility of perfect foreknowledge and the second does. Either way, human prayer is not regimented and God's response is not mechanically prescribed. Prayer can be freely chosen and efficacious, honored by both God and the one who prays, making the divine-human relationship genuine and personal. But allowing God to operate from controlled consciousness without curtailing His foreknowledge frees Him to become aware of whatever future petitions He might need to take into consideration.

A fifth operational area of God's non-conscious foreknowledge regards specific plans and purposes for His people. Strict advocates of foreknowledge often say that God could not formulate plans for a person that He knows will not be actualized. Proponents of Openness say God does not have foreknowledge of contingent future events, so He often purposes for us what we are free to veto. Here I also am saying that God can make plans for us that we are free to derail. But God's freedom to make plans for what may not be actualized is not grounded in His lack of knowledge but in His willingness to keep certain items of foreknowledge "out of mind" and operate in the world from successive occurrences. These plans are formulated in the context of time rather than timelessness. (They are not to be confused with those purposes which God may have for some persons that He intends to fulfill.)

In this view there is a difference between God's original choice for a person and God's optional choice. If the first choice is sabotaged, a backup plan is in place which becomes God's first choice under the new set of circumstances. In this way God is "hanging loose," "rolling with the punches" and subjugating His wishes to human choices. But it only requires a willingness not to function from foreknowledge, not a negation of foreknowledge. God can comfortably relate with the human situation if He keeps foreknowledge of certain contingencies out of consciousness.

Other Areas

Not only in these five areas but in all areas of interacting with contingencies in the world, God may function by keeping a portion of His knowledge out of consciousness. Openness theologians emphasize that God relates with the world sensitively, dynamically, with flexibility, vulnerability, generosity and caring concern. They stress that God is active in history and seeks to accomplish His purposes subtly and by personal influence, allowing human freedom. All of these conclusions about God's activity in the world are also drawn from the principle of selective consciousness without requiring a denial of absolute foreknowledge. This view does not say how much or how often God blocks items out of consciousness. It simply asserts that doing so is within God's prerogatives. And it allows God to have what Openness calls an "open" relationship with the world.

But the view that God is selectively aware of known future events has a distinct advantage over Openness. It places God in an auspicious position to access for instant awareness any future event to facilitate what is best for those He seeks to help. Openness theology, which denies God's foreknowledge of contingencies, is forced to allow that "it is always possible that even that which God in his unparalleled wisdom believes to be the best course of action at any given time may not produce the anticipated results in the long run," as David Basinger says.[7] This hazard can be avoided by a God who by infinite foreknowledge can factor future certainties into His present plans.[8]

Chapter 6

Omnipotence and Limitations

Throughout human history, even in pagan religions, deity has probably been perceived more in terms of power than any other attribute. In Greco-Roman tradition, Hercules, the son of Zeus, was adored because of his strength. Power commands respect, and an impotent god has little appeal.

The Judeo-Christian Scriptures define a God who is omnipotent—"omni-potent," all-powerful, with infinite strength, energy or might. Consequently one of His names is Almighty. God declared to Abraham, "I am God Almighty" (Genesis 17:1). The psalmist shouted, "Power belongs to God" (62:11). He sang of "the greatness of Thy power" (66:3) and declared, "He rules forever by his power (66:7, NIV). Isaiah proclaimed, "In the LORD JEHOVAH is everlasting strength" (26:4, KJV). Jesus said, "With God all things are possible" (Matthew 19:26). In the Apocalypse the elderly apostle heard heavenly hosts lifting their voices in an exultant shout: "The Lord God omnipotent reigneth" (19:6, KJV).

Nearly two centuries ago Adam Clarke wrote,

> Such is the potency of God, it can do all things that do not imply absurdity. . . . It can do anything in any way it pleases; it can do anything when it pleases; and it will

do anything that is necessary to be done, and should be done, when it ought to be done.... Everything is equally easy to the Power which is unlimited. A universe can be as easily produced by a single act of the divine Will as the smallest elementary part of matter.[1]

Centuries earlier Aquinas said, "God . . . infinitely abounds in active power."[2]

Process and Openness

In our day Process theology has introduced to us a God whose power is limited to manipulation and persuasion, a God who is a part of the universal system rather than Creator of the system. John Cobb writes, "There is no reason to suppose that the world once came into being out of nothing, or that any precise goal or unalterable, specific purpose has guided its development. The fact that theologians once thought this way is no reason to think so now." Then he adds, "God in every moment works with and upon the world that is given to him in that moment."[3]

Banking on Charles Hartshorne, Cobb strips away almighty omnipotence from the notion of divine power, and leaves an impotent God struggling to control a largely unmanageable universe by lobbying, persuading and manipulating through intermediate forces. "The power too often attributed to God," says Cobb, "is the power to compel or to force. But . . . the use of such power . . . expresses total powerlessness in all ways that matter. . . . The only power capable of any worthwhile result is the power of persuasion. . . . Persuasion is the means of exercising power upon the powerful."[4]

In response to this, Openness theology lifts a shield to defend traditional theism, asserting that God is indeed infinite in power, capable of bold strokes, sometimes acting unilaterally from sheer power. Having made this point, Openness joins

Process in emphasizing a sometimes neglected point in historic Christendom—that God more often does exercise power through persuasion and moves multilaterally in cooperation with His people. Pinnock says,

> God . . . may will to achieve his goals through agents, accepting the limitations of this decision. Yet this does not make God "weak," for it requires more power to rule over an undetermined world than it would over a determined one. Creating free agents and working with them does not contradict God's omnipotence but requires it.[5]

He asks, "Is God's power not as wonderfully displayed in his condescension to our weakness as in the starry heavens?"[6] Then Pinnock clarifies, "God's power is limitless but is deployed in ways that may appear weak."[7]

Some have pointed to two dimensions of God's power which may be called "elective" and "executive." The elective is His supreme creative power, the "intrinsic power of God's will . . . a voluntary self-energizing," says John Miley.[8] The executive dimension is the economical exercise of that power which often uses secondary agents or situations. The first is the "teleological" purpose of what is done and the second is the "efficient" cause. Many in the Church expect God to act independently, from "elective" power, overlooking His general "executive" policy of operating bilaterally or multilaterally, economically dispensing His power and including others in noble involvements. Openness thinkers have made the point strongly without sacrificing God's absolute omnipotence as Process theology has done.

Power and Ability

What is appalling is the loose way power is generally understood and the various meanings the phrase is often expected to cover. The word "power" is sometimes used to mean author-ity—power to control. It is sometimes used to mean potential—power to become. Frequently it is used to mean ability—power to accomplish.

While God does have awesome authority and ability, when the term power is applied to God it specifically means some-thing different from the above. The basic meaning of power is strength or energy, and it is in this sense that God's power is infinite. It is not primarily physical energy, of course, but mental energy and spiritual force, which created physical en-ergy in the universe at the beginning. God's power often includes skill or adroitness or dexterity or authority or ability, but the notion of strength is essential and it is in that sense that God is omnipotent.

Even a cursory look at standard theological works shows that God's power has generally been defined in terms of what He *can* do, and this is unfortunate. Real difficulty comes when we define God's power as *ability* and fail to realize the difference between the two. Omnipotence implies God can do anything that *is a function* of power. But some things are functions of other requirements and cannot be affected at all by power. Even infinite power cannot do what cannot be done. It should be obvious that infinite power does not entail infinite ability.[9]

Power is something that resides in a subject quite apart from the object, but ability never belongs to a subject independent of its relationship with the object. Whether an object is capable of being affected by the power contained in the subject says more about the object than the subject. No subject, regardless of its power, has the ability to do what cannot be done. In order for a subject to have the ability to affect an object, the object has to have the "ability" to be affected. If something cannot possibly be done, it cannot be done even by omnipotent power. And its "inability" to be done does not make God's power less than omnipotent. I have clarified this point in an earlier book.[10]

Non-theist logicians have sometimes argued deductively against the existence of the Christian God with a logic based squarely on the failure to distinguish between power and ability. The argument is formulated like this: If God were good He would want to eliminate evil, and if He were all-powerful He could do anything He wishes, but there is evil. Therefore, if God exists He is either not good or not all-powerful, either of which makes Him less than the Christian God.

The second premise of that argument—"if God were all-powerful He could do anything He wishes"—begins with power and ends with ability, equivocating ability from power. The premise contains the fallacy of equivocation. The idea of ability is not contained in power, but in this argument it rides piggyback on power. Then the conclusion that God is not all-powerful is deduced from ability rather than power, this time equivocating non-power from non-ability. God's inability to eliminate evil without withdrawing human freedom to produce evil does not reflect negatively on God's power. It simply shows that an omnipotent God does not have unlimited ability. Rebutting the non-theist argument obviously entails much more, but what I have shown here is basic.

That ancient argument about God being unable to create a stone too big for Himself to lift has been answered several ways, generally having something to do with the problem of contrary premises. But the argument can best be countered by recognizing the difference between power and ability. Lifting created stones is a matter of power. Creating stones that cannot be lifted is a matter of ability which has nothing to do with power. God does not have the ability to create an unliftable stone precisely because He has infinite power to lift any stone. He does not have infinite ability because He does have infinite power. In this sense His ability is limited by His power.

The claim of omnipotence is a claim that God can do anything that is a normal function of power. He can do whatever requires nothing more than power to be done. It is not a claim that God has the ability to do what cannot be done by power.

Logical Limitations

With this background we can understand three kinds of limitations on God's ability that cannot appropriately be considered limitations on His power.

First, God's ability is limited by logic. This is not to say that God does not have the power to think or act illogically. As an independent being God does have the freedom to act irrationally, though He by nature is prohibited from irrational acts because He is a logical, rational being—in the same way that He is self-constrained from unethical behavior because He by nature is morally good.

The kind of limitation by logic that I refer to is something different from thinking or acting illogically. Here I am referring to performing logical contradictions. Rather than a limitation on God, this is more a limitation on what can be done. To be able to perform a logical absurdity is to be able to do what does not have the "ability" to be done. It is a logical impossibility. Many Christian philosophers and theologians as far back as Aquinas have made the point that logical contradictions are not included in the idea of omnipotence.

No amount of power, for instance, can correlate mutual exclusives. Additional power will not help. The power of a dinosaur can come no nearer drawing a square circle than the power of an ant. A stick of dynamite has no more ability to draw a four-angled triangle than a firecracker, but it is much more powerful. Even omnipotent power cannot create a world which after its creation is an uncreated world.

Someone says God can draw a square circle by changing the definition of square and circle. But it is still the case that God does not have the ability to draw a square circle without changing the definition of one of the terms. That still leaves God with less than infinite ability.

What do we do then with Scriptures like: "Nothing is too difficult for Thee" (Jeremiah 32:17); "Behold, I am the LORD, the God of all flesh; is anything to difficult for Me?" (32:27); "With God all things are possible" (Matthew 19:26); "Nothing will be impossible with God" (Luke 1:37)? Do these lines mean God can do anything?

Here are three answers. First, the Scripture sometimes addresses certain situations in language that would be an overstatement if applied to all situations. The Bible uses hyperbole, not intended to be applied literally across the board to every situation. For instance, Jesus said one must "hate" one's father, mother, wife and children to be His disciple (Luke 14:26).

Second, the Bible makes many statements that are generally true, but it does not become laborious with meticulous disclaimers.

Third, because square circles, four-sided triangles and created worlds that are uncreated are intrinsically contradictory, they are not "somethings" to be done. They are "nothings" that cannot be done. They are nonentities. As nothings they could never possibly be somethings. If we are to be meticulously literal about the verses above, we must admit that each verse only says God can do any "thing"; it does not say He can do a "non-thing" that could not possibly be a thing. It is only nothings that God logically cannot do, not somethings. The Bible correctly says God can do anything. The Bible cautiously avoids saying God can do "nothings."

A large number of lay persons, however, point to miraculous occurrences in the New Testament to prove that God can perform acts that are logically contradictory. They claim the resurrection of Jesus demonstrates God's ability to do what is illogical.

Those who make the claim have confused logical law with

natural law, assuming that anything that is unnatural is illogical. A natural law points to a causal relationship between cause
and effect, but a logical law points to a logical relationship
between premise and conclusion. God created nature, so He
has the power to intercept or even violate natural law. Certainly
He is free to introduce transnatural causes into the natural
system to alter natural effects. This is what we call a miracle.

In a miracle God transcends natural law, but not logical law.
Logical laws are specific and precise—laws like simplification,
adjunction, *modus ponens*, constructive dilemma, exportation,
equivalence, distribution. There are some twenty of them. In
the resurrection of Jesus natural laws were manipulated, ad-
justed or broken. But not one logical law was touched. All
logical laws remained perfectly inviolate. There is nothing
illogical about a divine miracle.

God's inability to perform logical contradictions has special
implications in the trade-off between divine freedom and human freedom, as we will see later on.

Moral Limitations

God's ability is not only under logical limitations, but secondly, it is limited by *moral* principle. What God *can* do is a
larger category than what God *will* do. What He can do speaks
of His freedom; what He will do speaks of the self-limitations
of His character. A.H. Strong says, "God can do all he will, but
he will not do all he can."[11] Because He is morally constrained
from certain actions, God has greater power than ability. He
has power to do certain things that He is morally unable to do.

Scripture says, "Thou canst not look on wickedness with
favor" (Habakkuk 1:13). Referring to God's moral character,
Paul said God "cannot deny Himself" (2 Timothy 2:13). To Titus
Paul said God "cannot lie" (1:2) and Hebrews says, "It is impossible for God to lie" (6:18). James said, "God cannot be tempted
by evil" (1:13).

In those lines, the "cannot" and the "impossible" refer to character constraint rather than a limitation of power. It is appropriate to say God *cannot* do what He otherwise *can* do if we understand that the "cannot" refers to moral ability and the "can" refers to power. God "cannot" because He will not. And He will not because it would not be right.

A big difference stands between what God can do by might and what He can do by right. God's power or might has more to do with what He is as deity, but His moral character defines what He is as God—for goodness is included in our definition of God. As a metaphysical being God has freedom to commit sin, but as God He is prohibited by His own goodness.

We see the same operative principle in our own lives. We have free power to commit certain atrocious crimes that we nevertheless cannot do. We can, but we cannot. From power we can, but from conscience we cannot.

Whether God can commit sin is answered by whether you are referring to power or ability.

Those who generalize that God cannot sin often overlook the necessary place of moral freedom in the concept of moral goodness. In order to be morally good, any being requires freedom not to be good. If the being were a robot with no freedom, it would be morally neutral. An automaton may be functionally good, but it is morally neither good nor bad. In order for God to be morally good, He necessarily must have the power to be bad.

But because goodness is entailed in an appropriate definition of God, we can say that God as God cannot be morally evil without losing His "God-ness." As metaphysical deity He has freedom not to be good. As God He is constrained by character from being bad. It is like a young man who is free to get married, but he is not free to be married and remain a bachelor. As a person he is free to be married. As a bachelor he is not. As an all-powerful being, God is free to do evil. As God He is not.

Moral goodness limits God's ability to do evil while not reducing his omnipotent power.

Some controversy has arisen over the doctrine of the "impeccability" of Christ, which states that He could not have sinned while under temptation. The problem is resolved by determining whether the "could not" refers to His free power or to His moral character. From the standpoint of freedom Christ could sin, otherwise the temptation could not have been temptation. From the standpoint of His moral character, He was restrained by goodness. In regard to His moral nature it is correct to say He could not sin.

Self-imposed Limitations

Not only is God's ability under logical and moral limitations, but thirdly, it is under some self-imposed limitations.

Strong says, "Omnipotence in God does not exclude, but implies, the power of self-limitation."[12] Thiessen says, "God has power over his power."[13]

We observe God's self-limitation in the way He systemizes His activity in the world. Generally He functions systematically rather than haphazardly, restricting and disciplining His omnipotent power. God has a system of operation. Certainly His method is not inalterable. On occasion He acts arbitrarily, but even His choice to do so is guided by purposes that we may not be able to detect.

Though God may frequently make bold moves into natural law that we are not aware of, as a general rule He operates naturally inside the natural system. Before requiring Him to break out of natural law to prove His miraculous power, we should remember that the natural order is His system in the first place. He Himself created it to function by His natural laws. Whenever He breaks out of the system, for instance, in performing instantaneous acts of physical healing, He probably does so for systematic reasons rather than by caprice or random.

Openness theology stresses what I call God's self-limitation by pointing out the method God uses in deploying His power—"in the form of servanthood and self-sacrifice," Pinnock says. He insists that God's love is a higher quality than His power, and God exercises His power through love. "God does not go in for power tactics."[14]

God's self-imposed restrictions come into clearest focus where freedom is granted to His creatures, which we will consider more fully in the next chapter. Either we humans are mechanical robots deceiving ourselves in thinking we have some freedom to determine our actions, or God has actually given us a measure of self-determination.

At this point God's logical limitations "kick in." God cannot grant freedom and withhold it at the same time for the same person in the same area in the same way. It is a logical thing. Either our behavior is determined by our own free autonomy or by forces outside ourselves, which may include God. But the area that is self-determined is not God-determined—otherwise the notion of personal freedom is an illusion.

God's self-restriction is what largely governs or inhibits God's activity in human life. Rather than moving arbitrarily and unilaterally, God often chooses to subject His activity in our lives to our own willingness to align our choices with His purposes. He has power to impose His will on us, but He does not have the ability to prevent our decisions without withdrawing our freedom to make a decision. Because of logical necessity, God self-limited His ability in order to allow our freedom.

Chapter 7

Sovereignty and Freedom

When Jason Jones sneaked out with his father's hunting knife to play in the yard, the father rushed outside, gave the lad a spank and retrieved the knife. Doing so was no problem. Jason was only four, and his father was stronger in every way. Fifteen years later Jason, now broad-shouldered, virile and a black belt in karate, wanted to use his father's car. Mr. Jones replied, "I'm sorry, but I have a meeting tonight and I must have the car." And Jason did not get the keys.

The father did not have the strength to enforce the prohibition on so strong a son, but he did have the authority. The car belonged to him. Mr. Jones managed his own possessions both when Jason was a child and when he was an adult. Earlier he executed control by might. Now he did it by right.

The difference between omnipotence and sovereignty is the difference between power and authority. Power is something one has within oneself. Authority is something determined by one's position. It has to do with dominion over one's domain, official right of control over one's jurisdiction. Sovereignty is executive privilege by virtue of position. It is a matter of exclusive rights.

Since God is God, He not only has absolute power, but He

occupies a position of absolute authority. He is sovereign by virtue of His "God-ness." Sovereign authority is intrinsic to God for no greater reason than that He is God.

As an old man, David prayed, "Everything that is in the heavens and the earth; Thine is the dominion, O LORD" (1 Chronicles 29:11). A psalm says, "But our God is in the heavens; He does whatever He pleases" (Psalm 115:3). Even the heathen king Nebuchadnezzar said of the Hebrew God, "He does according to His will in the host of heaven and among the inhabitants of the earth" (Daniel 4:35). Paul said God "works all things according to the counsel of His will" (Ephesians 1:11).

God's right to require subordination from His creation does not come from His omnipotence. It comes from His sovereignty. It may be supported by power, but the right does not come from the power. If His sovereignty were not backed by His power, we would owe Him no less allegiance. If His right were stripped of His might, He would deserve the same obedience.

Calvinism and Arminianism

Christian theists traditionally agree that God is sovereign, but they disagree over the extent to which God's *activity* is governed by His sovereignty. The theological rift between Calvinism and Arminianism stems directly from this disagreement.

To hyper-Calvinists, sovereignty includes sovereign activity. Being sovereign implies acting from sovereignty. To allow others to engage in activity that is not sovereignly directed would imply God is less than sovereign. The five major points of classical Calvinism have been consistently deduced from that understanding of sovereignty. God determines by divine decree who will be eternally saved. They are given a choice, but the choice is so heavily influenced by God that it amounts to "determined" choice rather than free choice. It is what Calvinism refers to as "irresistible grace."

Arminians, on the other hand, hold that God can sovereignly choose not to act from sovereignty, not to control others by His sovereignty and not to determine sovereignly every detail of every possible occurrence. God is sovereign *enough* not to have to act from sovereignty. He does not have to exercise sovereignty or operate from sovereignty in order to remain sovereign. God is sovereign even over His own sovereignty.

Basic to the notion of divine sovereignty is divine freedom. Calvin said, "[God's] will is . . . the cause of all things that are. . . . God's will is so much the highest rule of righteousness that whatever he wills, by the fact that he wills it, must be considered righteous."[1] From this has come the exaggerated interpretation that God does not do anything because it is good, but it is good because He does it. William Ames declared, "[Predestination] depends upon no cause, reason or outward condition, but proceeds purely from the will of him who predestines."[2] Richard Watson interprets extreme Calvinists as saying that God's "sovereignty [means] his doing what he wills only because he wills it" rather than admitting that "this right is under the direction of his 'counsel' and 'wisdom'."[3] Extreme Calvinists seem to think that if God should act for any reason other than from sovereign freedom, His freedom would be limited and He would not be sovereign. Though they would hesitate to admit it, the view would seem to end up defining God's freedom as little more than impulse or whim. God's actions would function simply from caprice.

Arminians and moderate Calvinists could reply that God is even more sovereign than extreme Calvinists allow, that He is sovereign over His own feelings, desires and impulses, that He is free *not* to act from freedom alone, but to subject His actions to wisdom or rightness or long-range purposes. Genuine freedom includes freedom to self-impose constraints.

So far as we can see, God did not need to comply with any

moral principle in creating the world. In Revelation the living creatures sang, "Thou has created all things . . . for thy pleasure" (4:11, KJV). Yet even in creation we see God operating from wisdom: "The LORD by wisdom founded the earth; by understanding He established the heavens" (Proverbs 3:19). If God functions from wisdom, He does not function from uninfluenced sovereign freedom.

In other areas God operates from moral principle. He loves, executes justice and extends mercy because these are the right things to do. The psalmist appeals to God's moral goodness and says, "Remember Thou me, for Thy goodness' sake" (Psalm 25:7). As a metaphysical Being, God has sovereign freedom to act purely for what pleases Him. As moral God, acting on that sovereignty is modified by moral principle.

John Wesley argued that "the sovereignty of God is never to be brought to supersede His justice."[4] When we distinguish between God as sovereign Creator and as just Governor, "we shall give God the full glory of his sovereign grace without impeaching his inviolable justice."[5]

Certainly this does not suggest divided interests or a tug of war within God. Because He is good by nature, even His desires are so attached to His goodness that what pleases Him most is what is good. Hence the psalmist could say, "He does whatever He pleases" (Psalm 115:3). In conforming to goodness, God is doing what He wants to do. Even His sovereign desires are subject to moral value. Both His sovereignty and His goodness are categories under His "God-ness," without either of which He would be less than God.

Another restriction on the exercise of God's sovereignty is purely voluntary on God's part. It is at the point of granting human freedom. The way theists interpret God's use of His own sovereign freedom goes a long way in determining their views about human freedom.

Among non-theists we find a broad range of views about

human freedom. Philosophical determinists believe every thought, feeling, word and action of every person is mechanically determined by blind causes, leaving people with no freedom. Non-determinists hold that human behavior is pure random, chance or happenstance, neither determined by outside forces nor self-determined by human freedom. Compatibilists say that human behavior is both caused and chosen, without contradiction between the two. Libertarians hold that at least a measure of human action is freely chosen without outside constraint.[6]

Divine Determinism

Most theists embrace one of three different views about human freedom, determined largely by their view of divine sovereignty. The first we will call *divine determinism*. In this view God meticulously controls every detail of life including human thoughts, feelings and actions. Proponents of this view claim that perfect control even of trivial detail is required in order for God to be sovereign. To them, being sovereign entails acting sovereignly, which implies absolute control. If every minute detail of human life is under meticulous divine control, the obvious conclusion is that people have no freedom. They are mechanically controlled like robots. They may think they are free, but it is an illusion. They can move only when God chooses to move them. Like marionettes, they move only when God pulls the strings. Their freedom is preempted by God's freedom over them.

Because acting implies an actor to do the acting, whatever people do must be called behavior rather than human action.

Since human beings have no freedom, we would not expect them to be held responsible for what they are or what they do. They deserve neither praise nor blame. Either reward or punishment would be misplaced. Logically they are not culpable for wrongdoing.

Some proponents of divine determinism, however, have argued that evil people deserve punishment for being evil, even though they could not help being evil. Still they are evil, the argument goes, and being evil deserves punishment.

Something unwieldy about that argument arrests our attention. For one thing, it is unclear just how persons could be morally evil if they had no free moral choice. Without free choice they might have evil inclinations, but that is different from being evil. Without at least an element of moral freedom, they would be morally neutral, like an automaton, not morally evil. Even if they should be evil, it is unclear how they could be culpable if they could not help being evil. We are not "guilty" of being tall or short, or Caucasian or African American or square-jawed or narrow-nosed, because we cannot prevent it. If evil people could not keep themselves from being evil, they are not guilty of being evil. And if they are not guilty, even evil people are innocent of being evil. They may suffer as a consequence of what they are, but to suffer punishment for what they are would be a miscarriage of justice.

Another problem with absolute divine determinism keeps hounding us. Throughout the Bible we see God interacting meaningfully with people, responding seriously to their requests, involved dynamically with their lives. Though divine determinism would allow worship, devotion and adoration, it is hard to see how it could allow dynamic relationships and meaningful fellowship between God and mankind. Staged relationships have no spontaneity or responsiveness. For this reason both Process and Openness theology, as well as the best in classical theology, reject strict determinism.

Compatibilism

A second theistic view of human freedom is often called *compatibilism*. Among non-theists the word is used by those who hold that the notion of human freedom is compatible with naturalistic and psychological determinism. But many theists wish to embrace both human freedom and determinism, and the term is used to describe the effort to make the two compatible.

Both Martin Luther and John Calvin wished to leave God ultimately in absolute control, but they both recognized what appears to be an element of human freedom to make individual choices. Compatibilists attempt to reconcile what would otherwise be contradictory concepts, leaving God with meticulous control while allowing human beings the privilege of choosing. Aquinas appears to embrace compatibilism when he says, "God does not destroy our acts of freedom, indeed he causes them."[7]

Among proponents, compatibilism variously takes different forms. Some insist that persons have *no options*, that their "freedom" does not imply alternatives. They are "free" to comply with God's decisions, but they are not free not to comply. They choose, but they have no options to choose between. Their choice is free, but what they choose is determined. If God decrees for them not to be saved, they will choose to reject salvation because God chose for them to choose to reject. To choose to accept salvation is not an open option. Their freedom consists in their ability to do what they are forced to do. It is like the freedom of the hands of a clock to move across the clock's face.

The problem with this is that what is called freedom is not real freedom because the hands are under exact control. Freedom under those conditions is no more than a courtesy title, "in name" only. Coercion is not compatible with freedom; it is opposite freedom. Genuine freedom requires viable options and genuine alternatives.

Another compatibilist slant is that people have *no autonomy*, no creative freedom for self-direction. Their freedom is passive rather than active, what some would call outer freedom rather than inner. People are free *from* but not free *to*. They are free from obstructions and outer restraints, but not free to initiate action. In this sense water is free to flow uphill because there is no obstruction, but it has no creative ability to initiate such an action. An automobile is free to speed cross-country, but it requires a driver to initiate the movement, perpetuate it and direct it. People are "free" to do what they are unobstructed from doing, though they have no active ability to do it. Outwardly they "can" but inwardly they cannot.

To some of us, however, that is a loose use of the word "freedom," for genuine freedom entails active creative autonomy.

Still another compatibilist angle admits to personal autonomy, but insists that it operates exclusively by motivation. God determines every choice one makes because He controls the motivation. People can do anything they will to do, but they have *no will* apart from God's decrees.

Making human freedom compatible with divine determinism would be rather difficult if human choice were the direct effect of divine decrees. So compatibilists recognize secondary or intermediary causes through which God's primary causes operate. Human choices then become indirect effects of divine causes. At this point many theists have used the categories of behaviorism even before behaviorism was developed as a social science. A person's will is thought to be nothing more than intensified desire. People are expected to do what they want to do if they want to do it strongly enough. Human personality by nature makes choices consonant with motives, drives and incentives, as well as environmental conditioning and reinforcement. God controls human choices by controlling these human desires. God used behavior modification long before B.F. Skinner popularized the notion.

Though human beings in principle have creative ability to do otherwise, these compatibilists claim, in practice they are directed by whoever or whatever controls their desires. Freedom to do otherwise does not mean that they will do otherwise. By creating overwhelming desires, propensities and inclinations, God "stacks the deck" and "loads the dice" so heavily that for practical purposes it becomes determinative. Thus God decrees every choice all people will make while holding them accountable for making it.

Though we do observe people operating from desire, we note several problems with this view. For one thing, most people frequently have conflicting motives and desires, with diversified character inclinations influencing them toward opposing choices at the same time. Also, we often observe people making choices from principle rather than desire, selflessly sacrificing personal wishes in deference to moral value or the wishes of others. Some persons even make choices beyond their own character inclination, sometimes acting "out of character." To say all persons always operate only from desire is to oversimplify the situation and commit the fallacy of generalization. It casts doubts on the very notion of freedom which the theory intends to uphold.

Another problem with the view is that it depicts God as conniving to produce evil people while insidiously attempting to legitimize His desire to punish them under the guise of freedom. God becomes a sinister force for evil who opposes His own program of righteousness. This is utterly intolerable in the name of Christian theology. Pinnock says, "To say that God hates sin while secretly willing it, . . . to say that God loves the world while excluding most people from an opportunity of salvation, to say that God warmly invites sinners to come knowing all the while that they cannot possibly do so—. . . that is just a euphemism for nonsense."[8]

Compatibilist views, like divine determinism, leave human beings with no genuine freedom, and that preempts the possibility of meaningful fellowship with God. If God enters responsively into dynamic relationships with people as the Scriptures portray, they must be allowed a freedom beyond what compatibilism allows. The way God provides that freedom and the extent of it will be the burden of the next chapter.

My point here, however, is that God either does or does not allow or provide an element of genuine human freedom, and if He does, He is either not sovereign or His sovereignty must be defined in a way to allow for that freedom.

Libertarianism

A third theistic view, called *libertarianism*, allows real human freedom without compromising divine sovereignty. It allows God to judge sin openly without hiding behind a fabricated human freedom. And it allows divine-human interaction in an active relationship that is meaningful to both God and human people.

Here God's sovereignty is defined in terms of His position, His authority and His right to determine everything that He wishes—even His right to determine to allow people to determine a large measure of their lives. Human freedom is not innate; it is conferred. If God sovereignly decrees to allow people freedom to determine their choices and their destinies, it does not make God less than sovereign. Only a sovereign God could sovereignly allow people the privilege of freedom. Some classical theologians just could not "get" the notion of voluntary limits on sovereignty. I insist that it is not a modified view of sovereignty, but rather something entailed in the very notion of sovereignty.

To say that God grants human freedom is not to say that everybody operates from that freedom or that anybody always uses freedom. Some may act purely from desire, rarely using their freedom to act otherwise. But even then, they are using their freedom not to use their freedom, their freedom to go with the crowd or drift with the flow.

Nor do libertarians claim complete freedom for any person. We have freedom to walk out the door, but not freedom to walk through the wall. You can jog around the block, but not around the solar system. I can contribute a limited amount to charity, but not an unlimited amount. We can choose between available options, but not beyond those options. We can place ourselves in such a vulnerable position to temptation that it becomes virtually irresistible. We can become emotionally and psychologically incapacitated, unable to make responsible choices. Libertarians make no claim for absolute freedom, only for a measure of freedom.

To the extent God does grant human freedom, however, to that extent God self-limits His own freedom. Richard Rice says, "The will of God . . . is not an irresistible, all-determining force."⁹ God bows out of His freedom over people in the areas that He grants them freedom, though He may continue to influence and persuade. To the extent that He has granted them sovereignty over their own actions, He refuses to operate from His own sovereignty over them. In order to allow them freedom to choose, He voluntarily surrenders His freedom to determine their choices.

This gives us human beings the frightening ability to "handcuff" God (in restricted areas), to arrest His activity and to sabotage His purposes in our lives. We have been given the awesome freedom to lift rebellious palms against a sovereign God and refuse Him access to our lives.

Someone says, "Eventually God will send the sinner to hell, and that proves God will have His sovereign way." A closer look, however, shows it proves quite the opposite. The Scripture says, "The Lord . . . is patient toward you, not wishing for any to perish but for all to come to repentance" (2 Peter 3:9). Again the Scripture says, "God . . . desires all men to be saved" (1 Timothy 2:3-4). If a person separates him or herself from God, it proves that God does not get His way, that God is not operating from sovereignty over that person. As Wesley said, "You can bring no scripture proof that God ever did, or assertion that he ever will, act as mere sovereign in eternally condemning any soul. . . . "[10]

In a larger, broader sense, however, God remains free because the limit on His freedom is voluntary. Though as a general policy He chooses not to retrieve full freedom, God remains in a position to do so. He retains the right to intervene unilaterally in any person's life. Perhaps Pinnock comes on more strongly than he intends when he says, "God . . . jeopardizes his own sovereignty."[11] Though it may appear so to us, God's sovereignty itself is really not jeopardized. He is free over His own self-restrictions, to break out of those restrictions if He should so choose. To curtail His use of sovereignty is not to jeopardize His sovereignty. Sovereignty itself forever remains intact.

At this point Process theism has gone to the extreme, leaving a less-than-sovereign God without ability to move unilaterally in human affairs. Openness, though flawed, does correct that mistake, emphasizing God's sovereign ability to do as He pleases while voluntarily relinquishing a measure of freedom over human beings.

Chapter 8

Libertarianism and Its Implications

U ltimately, sovereignty belongs only to God. His is the only freedom with no outer restraints. In granting human freedom, God in a special sense made people like Himself. He has made us in His image, with freedom to determine (within bounds) our own choices, actions and destinies.

That has frightening implications, both for good and for evil. It entails both assets and liabilities that are beyond our grasp, both intellectually and emotionally. We are not adequately equipped either to contemplate or to feel its weightiness. This chapter will give a cursory overview of some of the implications of human freedom.

Accountability

First, people with moral freedom are morally accountable; they are deserving of rewards and punishment, and God is therefore justified in judging.

Having said that, we must realize that all of us have been so locked into personality patterns of self-centeredness, rebellion and rejection that we have lost the freedom to do a lifestyle about-face, an act which we call repentance. Compatibilists like Jonathan Edwards are correct that God must change human desires. Aquinas wrote that there can be "no conversion to God unless God turn us. To be turned to God is to be ready for grace. ... This we cannot do, without the free help of God in arousing us."[1] But Christian libertarians believe that God is constantly attempting to do just that, to activate a person's conscience and motivate the will. At that moment when a person is under the influence and motivation of God's Spirit, he stands at a moral fork in the road of life, with genuine freedom to choose either direction.

God is not a tyrant, arbitrarily refusing to choose some for salvation. Because He grants human freedom, God's sovereignty cannot be accused of tyranny. God functions as merciful Father ahead of sovereign ruler. He is the architect of a daring rescue operation to salvage all who will respond. John said that Christ is the "true light that gives light to every man" (John 1:9, NIV). And Paul said, "For the grace of God that brings salvation has appeared to all men" (Titus 2:11, NIV).[2]

Goodness

Second, having moral freedom gives one the opportunity to be morally good—and this has value for its own sake. Certainly God could create creatures with no freedom that still would have functional goodness to do what they were intended to do—like a good automobile. He could create beings with no freedom that would have utilitarian goodness to produce happiness—like a good drama or a good meal. He might even create conscious creatures with no moral freedom that would have propensities for kindness or generosity or other ingredients that we think of as morally good. This we find in many animals. But mere inclination toward qualities that we call morally good is quite different from *being* morally good. It is open to question whether God could create morally good people who had no moral freedom to choose to be good. It is true that we sometimes say that God created our primeval parents good, and the one prohibition gave them the opportunity to confirm their goodness. It is probably more accurate to say that He created them neither good nor evil, but with inclinations toward goodness and they only became good by choosing to obey. Entailed in moral goodness is the notion of morally good intent and that implies freedom to intend. Without moral freedom a person would be morally neutral.

Divine determinists generally hold that human goodness is exclusively "imputed," never actually "imparted," a "positional" goodness rather than "experiential." That is to say that God only looks through Christ at the redeemed as if they were good, but that they cannot even by God's grace become actually good. It is true that the biblical notion of atonement includes a "covering" for sin; that is what we call imputed goodness or justification. But evangelical libertarians generally note that the Bible comes down on the side of genuine goodness in addition to "accounted" goodness, that by God's regenerating grace we can have more than a provisional, pretended goodness. They hold that redemptive grace includes giving people at least a measure of moral rightness in addition to having a right "standing" before God, preparing people for heaven rather than simply herding them into heaven under the guise of goodness. This goes beyond justification and includes regeneration and sanctification.

In providing us with freedom, God allowed us to be like Himself, though in a very small way, in the area of His sovereignty. He gave us dominion over our choices. In providing us with *moral* freedom, He honored us with the opportunity to be like Him in a much greater way. In the area of moral goodness, He allows us to be Godlike. This is a privilege that cannot be claimed by either the natural or the animal order, so far as we know.

Moral Evil

Third, great assets entail grave liabilities, and the freedom that makes possible moral goodness requires the possibility of moral evil. With a taste of freedom, people wanted more. Sovereign over their own actions, they wanted to be sovereign over God. Some students interpret the Bible as implying the primeval sin was the effort to usurp God's position (Isaiah 14:12-14). Like their prehistoric parents in the Garden, people abused their freedom, crowded God out of their lives and determined to do as they pleased with no reference to moral principle. As part of a fallen race, they became little self-centered gods, gods that were not big enough to sustain them.

Consequently, a race of humans used its freedom in a way that enslaved them to pride, selfishness and sin. Their freedom was not intrinsic; it was derived. Therefore when they abused it, it turned on them and enslaved them. Freedom to sin became bondage. Sinners became more and more enslaved to selfish desires, evil patterns and egotistic appetites. Free people became enslaved in a way that would not be possible if they were not free.

If one defines hell as separation from God, then hell is freely chosen by those who do not wish to affiliate with God. Above I suggested that God is justified in judging evil people because they are morally culpable. The notion of divine punishment, though a biblical concept, may be redundant, however, to the notion of personal freedom to reject God. With its unthinkable atrocities, hell for the person who is debauched with self-centeredness may be preferable to the holiness, goodness, love and selflessness required in heaven. At least he has a psychological habitat that supports his evil disposition that he could never find in heaven. The presence of God would torture his conscience, disrupt his lifestyle and irritate his attitudes with intolerable torment. If he were trapped in God's presence, heaven would become "hell" to him.

In *Paradise Lost*, John Milton has Satan say to an underling, "Better to reign in Hell than to serve in Heaven."[3]

Suffering

Fourth, a relationship exists between freedom and pain, which we sometimes call utilitarian evil. A free-will theodicy may or may not account for all the suffering in the world, but it does account for a very large portion of human pain. Both natural freedom and moral freedom contribute, directly or indirectly, to physical, emotional and mental suffering, even though much of it may be innocent suffering. Because we live together in the same world as a human family, one's abuse of freedom causes pain for another. My freedom to hurt you is included in my own personal freedom. Without freedom to hurt I would not have freedom to help, which are optional sides of each other.

This is no claim for an easy solution to the problem of pain. Here we are discussing freedom rather than suffering, and the point here is that human freedom contributes to the pain of the world on a larger scale than we often know.[4]

Many otherwise libertarians are closet divine determinists at the point of human suffering. They think God should prevent all pain. When He allows a terrorist the freedom to bomb a building that kills innocent people, they come out of the closet to blame God. It is strange how we attribute so much to human freedom and natural causes until we suffer. Then we look for a divine purpose on which to pin the blame. We may question God's choice to allow human freedom under certain circumstances, but we must remember that we ourselves place a high priority on freedom. God may even have reasons to protect the freedom of evil people that we do not know. He obviously considers freedom to be something of great merit, even with its liabilities. Because of its overriding value, God has chosen to protect it even at the cost of pain.

Natural Effects

Fifth, entailed in divine sovereignty is the idea that God preserves the material world and universe by divine decree. Strong "preservationists" hold that God controls every aspect of the world every moment by constant manipulation, so that every natural occurrence, including earthquakes and floods, occur by divine order. Softer preservationists admit that God has frequent input into the natural system, but they see the world as having been programmed by God for preservation through the original creation. God preserves the universe through the "first cause." Aquinas wrote: "That God works in every active thing has sometimes been taken to mean that God alone, and no created power, produces real effects; for instance, that fire does not burn, but God does. This, however, is impossible.... It would argue weakness in God, for it is from strength that a cause gives to its effects the power of causing."[5]

Libertarians believe that God not only gives moral freedom to people but also a measure of natural freedom. If God preserves the world through a system of causes and effects, He has granted people the freedom to introduce causes into the system for natural effects. We can preserve the natural environment or rape it for economic purposes, neglecting rehabilitation and reforestation of strip mines and timbered lands. We can either enrich our soil or deplete it, control pollution or gag on it, use drugs for medicinal purposes or addictive indulgence. Libertarians like Richard Rice believe that "God's will is not the ultimate explanation for everything that happens."[6] By allowing human freedom, God is not directly responsible for every natural occurrence.

Similarly, we are granted natural input into the well-being of our physical bodies. We know many of the practices that damage our bodies and hasten death as well as those that prolong life. We can under-exercise, overeat, under-sleep, fill our lungs with nicotine, clog our veins with cholesterol, bake our emotions and fry our brains with narcotics. The consequence may not be a direct judgment from God; it may be a natural condition from having violated rules that govern the well-being of physical bodies. It is a peril whose possibility is entailed in freedom.

Relationship with God

Sixth, perhaps the primary reason God gave human freedom is for meaningful divine-human relationships. If we were under absolute divine control, we could have no more fellowship with God than characters of fiction have with their author. Meaningful relationships require love, and love by definition is something that is freely chosen.

Because people have genuine freedom in moral and spiritual areas, God can enter into serious interchange with them. Relationships with God can be lively, creative, dynamic and responsive rather than cold, calculated, formal and prescribed. God is "open" to human suggestions, decisions, attitudes and desires. Relationships are not closed because God is not closed to human initiative. Both the Process and Openness theologies, though flawed, have correctly insisted on libertarian freedom and a dynamically responsive God. Though Christian libertarianism has deep roots in a large area of classical theology, Openness theologians so emphasize it that they sometimes refer to their own theology as free-will theism.

Chapter 9

Transcendence and Omnipresence

O ne author creates his own characters of fiction from his creative imagination, while another writes essays narrating her own life story. The novelist transcends his creation, stands above it and is distinct from it. The autobiographer is identified with her story to the point she is a part of it. Fiction is a product of an author's creativity, but autobiography is an extension of an author's life.

This analogy, if not pushed too far, illustrates the difference between *transcendence* and *immanence*. The notion of a transcendent God is that He is distinct from the world He created, ontologically detached, of a different substance. Independent from the world, He stands in a Creator-creation relationship with it. In both existence and essence, He stands outside the material universe, transcending both natural and human processes. He created the world as a product of His creative autonomy but not as an extension of His nature, His substance or His being. God transcends the world in much the same way as a novelist transcends His work.

The idea of an immanent God is quite the opposite. He relates with the world more like an autobiographer relates with her narrative. God pervades the material universe, exists within it and is the big part of it, as she is the protagonist of her essays.

Deism and Pantheism

Two religious systems, deism and pantheism, have taken the notions of transcendence and immanence to extremes. Deism says that a transcendent God created the world to unwind itself through a system of natural laws and that it functions rather well on its own. It never needs outside manipulation, mechanical repair or mid-course correction. Since God is no longer needed by the world, He has become disinterested. He is now a distant God who does not relate with humankind, does not hear or respond to prayer and retains no particular interest in the direction or destiny of the world.

Pantheism has taken the immanence of God to the extreme in the other direction. God's relationship with the world is understood as a substantive relationship and therefore mechanically necessary. The world is an extension of God's essence. It is the substance of God. Consequently God's existence is understood to be in terms of the world. Every part of the universe is included in the beingness of God. By definition, God is "everything that is."

Western Pantheism holds that ultimate reality is material in nature (a view that is called materialism or naturalism), and the material world and universe thus comprise God. Eastern pantheism, on the other hand, holds that the substance of God and the world is nonmaterial (called idealism), which leads directly to pan-psychism and Eastern mysticism. Because everything and every person is of the same spiritual substance, every object is a part of God and every person is a spark in the divine flame. New Age philosophy attempts to incorporate Western humanism with Eastern pantheism to preserve individuality while reducing divine reality to human consciousness.

Relational Immanence

On first thought God's transcendence and immanence seem to be mutually exclusive, especially on the deistic-pantheistic model. God is either transcendent or immanent, but not both. To say He is both detached and connected at the same time, both independent and dependent, seems contradictory. Yet in the Judeo-Christian Scriptures we see God as both transcendent and immanent. What initially may seem incongruous, however, does not strain credibility when one realizes that God's immanence is relational rather than substantive. If God were immanent in the same way that He is transcendent, it would be contradictory. But if He is immanent in a different way, there is no problem. God's identity with the world is a relational identity, never substantive. Unlike pantheism, the Christian God is *substantively* transcendent, and unlike deism He is *relationally* immanent.

While ancient Greek philosophy generally affirmed the transcendence of God, ancient Hebrew religion depicted God as transcendent Creator. The Bible's very first line is a strong declaration that God is Creator, implying His distinction from the world and transcendence above the world. But certain Scriptures suggest God is also immanent. To Jeremiah, God declared His transcendence in a rhetorical question, but added His relational immanence at the end: " 'Am I a God who is near,' declares the LORD, 'and not a God far off? Can a man hide himself in hiding places, so I do not see him?' declares the LORD. 'Do I not fill the heavens and the earth?' " (23:23-24). Isaiah proclaimed, "Thus says the high and exalted One who lives forever, whose name is Holy, 'I dwell on a high and holy place, and also with the contrite and lowly of spirit' " (57:15).

When the Church fathers attempted to combine the salvation aspects of God with His universality and transcendence, they were not so much attempting to reconcile the biblical God with philosophic reflection. They were attempting to understand and lace together the various aspects of God that the Bible actually taught. The Scripture puts together transcendence and immanence, divine difference and relational closeness, in a unique package which it attributes to God. His transcendence inspires our worship and His immanence commands our devotion. And His transcendental "beyondness" makes the closeness of His fellowship more valuable.

Process and Openness theologians accuse traditional Christian thinkers of accenting God's transcendence to the point of curtailing His relational involvement with humankind. They are accused of emphasizing God's immutability, sovereignty, infinity and impassivity to support His transcendence while sacrificing His interaction with human life on earth. Reacting against these perceived extremes, both Process and Openness theology have strongly reasserted the immanence of God, but they have done it in different ways. Process has sacrificed transcendence and accentuated God's substantive immanence. Openness has stressed His relational immanence without having to sacrifice His transcendence.

Process Thought

In the last half of the twentieth century Process theism[1] has developed an unorthodox theological system with considerable contemporary appeal. Based on Whiteheadian metaphysics, Process theology has parted from historic Christian theism by declaring God to be less than transcendent. Alfred North Whitehead developed a complex ontology in which God is a part of the space-time dimension. What we know as material matter is a product of a "spatially extended continuum" in a "nexus" of occasions. Mind is a product of a "temporally extended continuum." So both material matter and mind are locked into and dependent on space and time. God's bipolarity, consisting of both a physical and a mental pole, is a product of space-time. The mental pole is God's primordial nature, something like a "Platonic form," which is pure potentiality waiting to be actualized. The physical pole is God's consequent nature, which is actuality. In His actuality we find God's immanence in the world. The material universe is actually God's domain. God's primordial nature, which presumably parallels transcendence, has no actuality.[2]

Like pantheism, Process philosophy makes God to be of the same substance as the world, divesting Him of transcendent existence. Process theology attempts to add theism to pantheism in a "divine relativity" that Charles Hartshorne calls pan*en*theism.[3] Either way, God is void of transcendence. He is an immanent God. Though God's immanence is substantive, it nevertheless accommodates divine-human relationships. So God is relationally immanent *because* He is substantively immanent. Unlike deists and what Process perceives to be the position of classical theism, Process theology sees God as involved in the world and relating dynamically with people, but He has no transcendence. He is not far enough ahead of us to be totally reliable, does not have adequate power to solve our problems and is without the transcendence to inspire worship.

Immensity

The transcendence-immanence dichotomy has its counterpart in another set of terms. While transcendence and immanence depict God's relationship with the material universe, and eternality and temporality show His relationship with time, *immensity* and *omnipresence* describe God's relationship with space. Since space as I have earlier defined it and the material universe are interrelated, in this chapter I am showing how God is omnipresent in space without violating His transcendence of the universe.

Because we *homo sapiens* are locked into a three-dimensional spatial context, we insist on conceptualizing God in the same way. "Where is God?" has long been a standard question. We get the feeling that God would be more real if we could locate Him on a map. We address God as "our Father in heaven," and Jesus over and again referred to God as "heavenly" Father (Matthew 6:14, 26, 32; 15:13; 18:35; Luke 11:13). Traditionally we have thought of heaven as located upward, but now we know that "up" simply means in a direction away from the center of the earth. Locating God "up in heaven" positions Him for Americans in an opposite direction from His position for Koreans. Even Jesus spoke of "ascending" into heaven and "descending" from heaven (John 3:13). We usually have no problem with the metaphorical use of the concept, however, for we commonly use the term "up" metaphorically as often as literally.

John A.T. Robinson, bishop of Woolwich, tried to make a case against what he called the "three-decker universe"—heaven above, earth beneath and waters under the earth. God is not "up there" nor "out there," he claims, but rather "in there," referring to the human spirit.[4] For Jurgen Moltmann, God is not above us, below us, within us or behind us, but rather ahead of us.[5] From these examples we see that attempting to locate God can be a slippery activity.

Just as transcendence speaks of God's detachment from the world and eternality describes His separation from time, the term "immensity" has been used to express God's essential separation from space. When the Samaritan woman wondered whether God should be worshiped in the mountain or in Jerusalem, Jesus answered that "God is spirit" and worship must be "in spirit" (John 4:20-24). Here Jesus underscores God's realm of existence as something other than the measurable universe and God therefore cannot be confined to our spatial dimensions.

Before Solomon began constructing the temple, he exclaimed, "But who is able to build a house for [God], for the heavens and the highest heavens cannot contain Him?" (2 Chronicles 2:6). When the temple was completed, Solomon in his dedicatory prayer said, "Will God indeed dwell on the earth? Behold, heaven and the highest heaven cannot contain Thee, how much less this house which I have built!" (1 Kings 8:27; see 2 Chronicles 6:18).

God's immensity means that He is infinite in relation to space and that He cannot be contained in any measurable frame. He is without measurable extension; He is above space, not circumscribed by it. God's essence is neither diffusible nor expandable. It is not spatially limited. God's magnitude cannot be calculated in centimeters, miles or light-years.

Some theologians have said that what we know as space is derived from God's immensity; it is a condescension, a "condensation," a "focusing down" of immensity, as time is a derivative of eternity. Strong says, "God is not in space. . . . Space is in God. . . . With creation, space began to be."[6] Immensity is not an extension of space any more than eternity is an extension of time. For both, the reverse is true. Orton Wiley says, "As time is born out of eternity, so space is born out of immensity."[7] Millard Erickson says, "God is the one who brought space into being. He was before there was space."[8]

Omnipresence

Earlier I have said that an infinite God is intricately cognizant of the infinitesimal, a timeless God is comfortably involved in successive temporal occurrences and a transcendent God is relationally immanent in the world. In a comparable way, an immense God who occupies a dimension that defies spatial positions condescends to express His presence at every point within space.

In Psalm 139 the psalmist first said God is here, in this place: "Thou hast enclosed me behind and before, and laid Thy hand upon me" (139:5). Then he said God is in every place:

95

Where can I go from Thy Spirit?
   Or where can I flee from Thy presence?
If I ascend to heaven, Thou art there;
   If I make my bed in Sheol, behold, Thou art there.
If I take the wings of the dawn,
   If I dwell in the remotest part of the sea,
Even there Thy hand will lead me,
   And Thy right hand will lay hold of me. . . .
When I awake, I am still with Thee. (139:7-10, 18)

Isaiah said, "He is near" (55:6), and Paul at Mars Hill declared, "He is not far from each one of us" (Acts 17:27).

The analogy of the sun being located at a place and sunshine covering the entire face of the earth gets some support from Psalm 113:4-6: "The LORD is exalted over all nations, his glory above the heavens. Who is like the LORD our God, the One who sits enthroned on high, who stoops down to look on the heavens and the earth?" (NIV). But the analogy is hardly appropriate to other Scriptures that portray God as being actually present, for sunshine is not the sun, and being in God's sight or under His smile is hardly the same as His immanent presence. Of course, we must admit the possibility that God in His nonspatial realm may occupy a position that would be analogous to what locality is in our realm. That kind of thinking, however, is beyond us. In our system of space as we know it, God is situated at every mathematical point—precisely because He is nonspatial. His other-dimension does not preclude His presence in this dimension. Rather He is able to be meticulously present in space because He is not spatially confined. God's omnipresence requires and presupposes His immensity.

Unless used metaphorically, terms like "here," "there," "where," "somewhere," "anywhere," "everywhere," refer to spatial location. Because God's existence is not native to space, it would be appropriate to say He does not exist any*where*—i.e.,

He is not localized in space, He breaks out of spatial limitations and He exists beyond space. But because God stoops to penetrate and occupy space, it is appropriate to say God is everywhere. At no place is He inaccessible. Omnipresence does not mean God is substantively included in everything, but it does mean He is not relationally excluded from anything. Because God is everywhere, the phrase "over there" is hardly in His vocabulary. Wherever God is, is "here" to Him. Since God is timeless, every time with God is now. Similarly, since He is space-less, every place to God is here.

A heathen philosopher queried a Christian, "Tell me, where is your God?" The Christian replied, "First, you tell me where He is not!"

Two important points need to be made about divine omnipresence. First, because omnipresence refers to God's presence within space, it is not an intrinsic attribute of God. God is not bound to the universe, so omnipresence is sometimes called one of God's relative attributes rather than an absolute attribute. His is not a substantive presence, as a part of the world. It is an operative, relational presence. God is inside the trunk of a tree, not as a part of its substance discoverable by a woodsman, but as an "outsider" whose attendance is voluntary rather than required. Aquinas said, "God is in all things, not, indeed, as part of their essence, nor as an accident, but as an agent is present to that upon which it acts."[9]

Since omnipresence refers to God's presence in space, if the universe were destroyed, taking all space fields with it, God's omnipresence would cease to be. Just as God could not be present in my desk drawer if I did not have a desk drawer, He could not be spatially present if there were no space. God's presence in space requires space for His presence. Without it, God would lose omnipresence without any diminishing of Himself.[10]

Second, the picture of omnipresence is not that God is so

massive that He fills all of space. If that were the case, each of us would have access only to that small portion of God nearest us. Rather, the idea of omnipresence is that God exists as a whole Person at every mathematical point in space at every moment of time. God's substance is incorporeal, spiritual, and as such He is undivided and undiluted, existing everywhere as a complete whole. So I have access to God's undivided attention and total presence in my home at the same moment that you have total access to God in your home a thousand miles away.

In an earlier chapter I said that God's timelessness can be elucidated either by saying all past and future occurrences are present to God, or by saying that He is every moment present in all the past and future. Similarly, we might understand the omnipresence of God either by saying He is present at every point in space or by saying that every point in space is present with Him.

When I stand at the classroom lectern, I am accessible to each student and each student is accessible to me. With my classroom amplifier I have presence with those near the back as well as those at the front. And with my good eyesight, those near the back are more present to me than some of them might wish. While we in the classroom do have spatial relationships, space is not a problem. I am immediately before them and each of them is immediately before me.

Whether God is present at every spatial point or every point is present to Him, presence is presence, and either way God is omnipresent. Both pictures portray the same thing.

Chapter 10

Constancy and Changeableness

Without being consulted to determine their wishes in the matter, human beings were placed in a changing environment to live changing lives in changing bodies within the context of a changing culture. Some changes are slow but steady. Others are sharp and cataclysmic.

Human emotions are relentlessly demanding. They require continuity with the past for emotional security, yet they need variety, change and discontinuity for creative fulfillment. Environmental flux is destabilizing, and sameness is tiring and dull. Without permanence people are disquieted, and without novelty they are bored. They need a God who is constant and unchanging while at the same time spontaneous, creative and active.

Is God a Constant?

Yet the notions of divine constancy and divine changeableness seem to be contradictory. God is either immutable or subject to change, but if He is either He cannot be the other. Whether God is changeable or unchangeable is a problem that has divided both theologians and philosophers as far back as ancient philosophy. Without the benefit of revelation, early Greeks had God's immutability "set in stone." He was immobile, sterile and inert. Some have interpreted Aquinas as thinking God's changelessness would necessarily preclude the possibility of personal involvement and meaningful relationships with people.[1] Responding to human beings would mean a change in God's experience, which would be disconsonant with the notion of a constant God. In order to allow God to be relational and responsive, some discarded the notion of immutability and cast God in a changeable mold.

Many theologians have overlooked a finer logical perception, however, that constancy and variableness are contradictory only if God is constant and variable in the same way or in the same area. But if He is changing in a different way from the way He is unchanging, the two ideas are compatible. Mainstream orthodox theologians today generally agree that God is immutable in some ways and changing in others. God is unchanging in His character, in His purposes and in His essence, which includes His attributes. Immutability is therefore not an attribute of God, but a characteristic of all His attributes. Anselm said that "in no respect art Thou unlike Thyself."[2] Yet these same theologians variously list areas in which God does "change," including movement in His "dealings with men," in His "treatment of His creatures" and in "the sphere of expediency," all of which speak of God's changing activities. Yet can we be justified in saying God is "changing" by pointing simply to His changing activities?

Process Theology

Process theology parts company with traditional theology at the point of divine immutability. Built on Whitehead's metaphysics of change,[3] Process theism requires God by nature to be in the process of change, otherwise He could not even exist.

Process metaphysicians locate ultimate reality in neither

mind nor spirit nor matter; to them the one irreducible entity is change, or activity, or experience, or event. Building blocks for everything that exists are "actual occasions" or "drops of experience." What we know as both mind and matter are products of the "actual entity" of change.

Process has its roots in pre-Socratic Greek philosophy. Heraclitus located ultimate reality in the *motion* of fire, which he called the clash of opposing opposites. Protagoras is known for his definitive statement, "All is becoming." Here he uses "becoming" not as a participle describing "all," but as a gerund synonymous with "all." The essence of everything is change, or process, or "becoming." To Process metaphysics, all being is defined in terms of becoming.

Something obviously awkward about this grabs our attention and demands an explanation. For one thing, Process thinkers are saying there is nothing at all that is permanent—*except* impermanence! Everything is forever in change, so only change is unchanging. So we end up with a constant in the universe after all, the constancy of inconstancy. The one invariable is variableness. Thus the philosophy requires a proposition that contradicts its basic tenet.

Another problem is even more clumsy to manage. Change is one of those nouns that is used to designate an active verb, but the verb cannot be active without a subject to do the acting. Change cannot exist of itself, on its own. Walking cannot take a stroll down the street; a walk requires someone to do the walking. Experience does not float around in the air. It requires someone to have the experience. Activity requires someone to act. There can be no change without something to change. And that something is logically prior to the change, and therefore more basic. How ultimate reality can be exclusively the fact of change is an enigma that defies rationality.

Process theology, based on that ontology, has also drawn from Georg W.F. Hegel's dialectical unwinding of the Absolute

Mind or Spirit in terms of thesis, antithesis and synthesis, which requires constant activity from the dialectical tension. It also grows out of Henri Bergson's idea of a growing and developing God.

To Process theism God, as well as everything else that is real, does not consist of an unchanging essence but of changing activities. John Cobb says, "The things of which everything else is composed, are energy-events. . . . Energy-events themselves are the ultimate reality. . . . Each energy-event is indissolubly spatiotemporal."[4] Being composed of changing activities does not make God impersonal, but as a person He is grounded in change.

Classical theologians like Aquinas viewed God as being 100 percent actuality, which meant He had no potentiality at all. As perfect absolute Being, He was incapable of becoming. Any change in God would have to be either for the better or for the worse, either of which would mean He was less than perfect. Aquinas wrote: "God . . . must be pure act, without the admixture of any potentiality. . . . Hence it is evident that it is impossible for God to change in any way."[5] Any movement within God from potentiality to actuality would mean that prior to the movement He was less than absolute actuality, which would be an inferior state. Traditional theologians did not allow such a mediocre God.

Then comes Process theology declaring God is both potentiality and actuality, constantly moving from the first to the second, and therefore always in the process of becoming. As actuality, He is locked into space-time, undergoing the constant change that all space-time beings know. He is as dependent on the world as the world is dependent on Him. Process theologian Schubert Ogden says God is "a genuinely temporal and social reality, and therefore . . . radically different from the wholly timeless and unrelated Absolute of traditional theism."[6]

As a changing God, He is able to accommodate the human

need for variety and creative fulfillment, and He can enter into changing relationships with people as they change. But He is not reliably in charge of the universe, does not hold the future in His hand and leaves people without the security of constancy, continuity and immutability.

Openness Theology

Like Process theism, advocates of Openness theology stress the changeableness of God which makes possible a dynamism in divine-human relationships. But unlike Process, they affirm the immutable character of God's nature and essence. Richard Rice speaks of "the constancy of God's character, not the content of his experience,"[7] and he distinguishes between "God's unchanging nature and his dynamic experience."[8] Clark Pinnock says, "God is unchanging in nature and essence but not in experience, knowledge and action."[9] The primary emphasis of Openness, however, is on the areas of God's changeableness as a corrective to what it considers to be a strait-jacketed, unyielding overemphasis on God's rigid immutability by traditional theology. While the practical conclusions of Openness in terms of God's relationship with the world are commendable, two problems are worthy of note.

First, traditional Christian theism is unfairly caricatured as interpreting God's immutability to mean He is inert, immobile, sterile and inactive. Rice says, "Everything about God must be changeless for traditional theism, whereas the open view sees God as both changeless and changeable."[10] Though some rigid classical theologians have held such strong views, they do not have a corner on traditional theism. Arguing against traditional theology on these grounds is to oppose a straw man.

Even Augustine, probably contradicting some of his other lines, spoke of God as "unchangeable, yet . . . all-renewing" (sometimes translated "yet changing all things"). And he said, "Thou changest Thy words, Thy purpose unchanged" (otherwise translated "changest Thy ways, leaving unchanged Thy plans").[11]

Though Aquinas held that God was pure actuality without potential, Aquinas never allowed this notion to preclude divine activity. Aquinas scholar David Burrell of Notre Dame University argues that the unchangeableness of Aquinas' God "does not entail his being inert, unresponsive or aloof."[12] Aquinas himself said, "God . . . does more for us than we can conceive."[13] Though the Thomistic God was not changed by His relationship with the world, He did nevertheless relate with the world (in a way that will be explained in the next chapter).

More recent theologians in the traditional stream have defined similar limits on divine immutability. Richard Watson said, "We are not to interpret the immutability of God as though his *operations* admitted no change, or even no contrariety; or that his mind was incapable of different *regards* and *affections* toward the same creatures under different circumstances."[14] Strong says, "Immutability is consistent with constant activity."[15] Miley says, "Change within the sphere of expediency is entirely consistent with the unchangeableness of God."[16] Thiessen says, God must "change his dealings with changing men in order to remain unchangeable in his character and purpose."[17] Wiley says immutability is "not a rigid sameness of being, but a characteristic of free intelligence."[18]

In reading Openness authors, I keep getting the feeling that they are more in the traditional stream, in many ways, than they are willing to admit.

A second problem with Openness is the insistence that God's changing activities and relationships constitute a change in God Himself. John Sanders asks, "Does not the act of creation itself imply a change in God?"[19] Hasker says, "When God began to create the world he changed."[20] Perhaps we have a semantic misunderstanding, but a distinction needs to be made between change in a person and change in a person's activity. The second need not imply the first. Variable activity means change in what a person *does*, not in what a person *is*.

Scriptural View

The Scriptures contain strong statements about the change-lessness of God. Israel sang, "Of old Thou didst found the earth; and the heavens are the work of Thy hands. Even they will perish, but Thou dost endure; and all of them will wear out like a garment . . . and they will be changed. But Thou art the same, and Thy years will not come to an end" (Psalm 102:25-27). Repeating the same lines, the New Testament declares, "The heavens . . . will perish, but Thou remainest. . . . Thou art the same, and Thy years will not come to an end" (Hebrews 1:10-12).

The last minor prophet quotes God as saying, "For I, the LORD, do not change" (Malachi 3:6). James speaks of "the Father of lights, with whom there is no variation, or shifting shadow" (1:17). And Hebrews says, "Jesus Christ is the same yesterday and today, yes and forever" (13:8).

Yet divine immutability refers to what God is within Himself, not to what He does. It has to do with God's character, His nature, His personhood, not His experience or activity. The Bible opens its first chapter with a beautiful account of God's creative experience. He can engage in an infinite variety of creative activity without affecting His unchangeable nature. Being immutable does not mean being immobile. To be stable does not mean to be static. Creative expression flows ceaselessly from His inexhaustible richness without altering His unchangeable character. Wiley says, "God is the same after creation as before . . . undiminished by the free overflow in creation."[21] Since it is God's nature to be creative, He is creative not in spite of His unchanging nature but precisely because of it.

Judeo-Christian faith proclaims a God who embodies both constancy and activity in a delicate balance, a God who is

105

unchanging without being dormant and creative without changing.

How then do we interpret the portions of Scripture that suggest God repented or changed His mind? Do they imply that God's intentions change and His purposes are volatile? God told Balaam to declare to Balak, "God is not a man, that He should lie, nor a son of man, that He should repent; has He said, and will He not do it? Or has He spoken, and will He not make it good?" (Numbers 23:19). Samuel said to Saul, "He is not a man that He should change His mind" (1 Samuel 15:29). The writer of Hebrews speaks of "the unchangeableness of His purpose" (Hebrews 6:17).

Yet other Scriptures at first seem to suggest that God did on occasion change His mind. After the human race fell into sin, the Bible says, "The LORD was sorry that He had made man on the earth" (Genesis 6:6). When Saul sinned, "The LORD was grieved that He had made Saul king over Israel" (1 Samuel 15:34, NIV). After God had declared He would destroy Nineveh (Jonah 3:4), when they turned from their evil ways "God relented" and did not destroy the city (3:10). In response to Abraham's petition, God did not destroy Sodom (Genesis 18); honoring Moses' prayer, God "relented and did not bring on his people the disaster he had threatened" (Exodus 32:14, NIV).

How do we reconcile what seem to be conflicting Scriptures? Because God chooses to be sincerely involved with humankind, He voluntarily makes both His feelings and His actions vulnerable to human activity. Being "sorry" that He had made man and being "grieved" that He had made Saul king over Israel do not suggest that God would have done otherwise with advance knowledge. They simply show that God responds emotionally in a way that is appropriate to the occasion. He is not emotionally aloof. Changing emotional states is consistent with an unchanging character, even required by it when the objects of emotion change. A change of feeling is not the same as a change of mind.

God's refusing to destroy Nineveh illustrates again that God often voluntarily allows human activity to determine His own activity in response. He allows His actions to be attached to human actions.

God's threat to destroy the city was given as a warning rather than as a sentence. When a parent scolds a child with "I'll spank you," the child understands the unstated condition: "if you do not quit what you are doing."

When an unchanging God enters into relationships with changeable people, the way He deals with them is necessarily determined by what they are. He cannot relate with an incorrigible rebel in the same way that He relates with a devotee. His relationships therefore change as His people change in order for Him to remain unchangeable in His character. The psalmist said, "The lovingkindness of the LORD is from everlasting to everlasting *on those who fear Him*" (Psalm 103:17, italics added). Assuming people sometimes change, God's changing relationships are required by His unchanging character. When the God who cannot repent (Numbers 23:19) did repent (Jonah 3:10, KJV), the contradiction is only in appearance. The first repent refers to character change and the second to relationships. The second repentance is required by God's non-repentance in the first.

In Jeremiah, God specifically states His policy of changing courses regarding people when they either become evil or become good (18:7-9). If God intends to alter His actions toward people as they change, doing so is not a shift in His intentions. In the case of Nineveh, God was operating on policy.

God's refusing to carry out His warnings in deference to the pleas of Abraham and Moses demonstrates again God's positive response to those who made the prayers. He prioritized His positive relationships with His devotees over His negative relationships with the rebels—since doing both in these cases would be mutually exclusive. Prayer does not change God's mind; it only alters His actions. He already wishes to respond to the pleas of His children.

In all these instances mentioned above, God's eternal character principles which do not change are applied to variable temporal situations with consistency, like an unchanging principle of physics is consistently applied to various substances in ways appropriate to each substance. God's relational activity necessarily changes because His character principles are eternal.

Theological mutations have not succeeded in changing God. A changing universe is attached to a constant. We have the security and reliability of His permanence. And His dynamic relational activity makes life for us creative and dynamic. Immutable and eternal while responsive and relational, God provides for us the best of both worlds.

Chapter 11

Independence and Relationality

B eing human can be a humiliating experience. We arrogantly take for granted those items that fulfill our basic human needs until we are deprived of them. Then we discover that we are not self-sustained. Our need for air, food, water and friends can only be met outside ourselves. We are dependent beings.

Our dependence on the natural environment is acutely symbolic of our greater dependency on God—in two primary areas. First, our *existence* has its source outside ourselves. We did not appoint our own committees to determine whether or when we would be born. Our lives have not been self-determined. For our existence we are dependent on God. Second, our *fulfillment* has its source beyond ourselves. Only when we adopt the purpose *behind* our lives for our primary purpose *in* life can we find genuine satisfaction.

We are neither self-caused nor self-fulfilled. As creatures rather than Creator, we are dependent on God to resolve our crises both in identity and in meaning.

Having become accustomed to our own dependence, we have difficulty thinking of any being that is totally independent. But historic theology has taught that God is absolutely independent. God said to Cyrus, "I am the LORD, and there is no other; besides Me there is no God" (Isaiah 45:5). To Israel God said, "To whom would you liken Me . . . and compare Me, that we should be alike? . . . For I am God, and there is no other; I am God, and there is no one like Me" (46:5, 9).

In both primary areas of our human dependency, God is independent.

Self-existent

First, God is independent in His existence. "Whatever God is," says A.W. Tozer, "and all that God is, He is in Himself. . . . The life of God is not a gift from another."[1] Complete within Himself, nothing else is necessary for God's existence.

Process theology radically departs from historic theology in making God interdependent with the world. Whitehead said, "It is as true to say that God creates the world as that the world creates God."[2] The implication is that the world also creates God as much as God creates the world. Ogden uses human beings as analogues of God in the area of self-knowledge. He points out that self-consciousness comes through the sense experience of one's own body. For any conscious being, selfhood is empirical, developing through temporal experience. Based on Whitehead's definition of mind as a "temporally extended continuum," Ogden says temporality is required for self-knowledge. God's actual sphere of existence is temporal experience. God knows Himself through the world, and is therefore dependent on the world.[3]

That is a reaction against neo-Platonism which maintains that the world is dependent on God in the sense that it emanates from God, and that both material and mental energy in the world flow from God's being. But rather than simply making the world dependent on God, Process makes God and the world interdependent. Both God and the world are processes in the same system, so each flows from the other. Neither is independent. Both God and the world are mutually necessary to each other.

The orthodox position of God's independence is somewhat difficult to form into an idea, because everything we experience in the natural realm is an effect from a prior cause. Even accidents are caused, though they are not purposed. We refer to them as accidents because they are not intended, but we never think of an accident as uncaused. Natural sciences like physics, chemistry, biology and electronics are developed on the assumption that there are no chance happenings. Nor do we consider God to be a product of random happenstance, so we naturally assume that He must be caused. Locked into our experience of causation, we are hard put to conceive otherwise. Consequently some theologians say God is self-caused or self-created rather than uncaused. They use the word "aseity," which means self-caused. This move prevents God's existence from being a chance happening without violating the principle of causation to which we have become conceptually enslaved.

Not Self-caused

We have a problem, however, in maintaining that God is self-created or self-caused. The notion of creating does not begin with a cause but with a purpose which is uncaused. It requires a condition of autonomous freedom, but the freedom is not a cause. In the process of creating, the uncaused purpose becomes a cause for that which is created. When we say God "willed" the worlds into existence, we are saying "final causation" became "efficient causation"—the purpose became the cause. But the purpose itself is uncaused.

When someone says God is self-caused, we assume that person means God purposed His own existence. This would ground God's existence in His will rather than in His nature. He would exist simply because He purposes to exist. But when one speaks of purposing, that requires someone to do the purposing. And that assumes an existence logically prior to (not temporally prior to) the existence that it purposes.

That not only defies analysis, but it implies the ability to self-destruct, which would make God capable of suicide. But if God's existence is a requirement of His nature rather than an intentional effect that He chose to cause, He is uncaused rather than self-caused. Then He cannot effect His own demise.

Strong says, "It is his nature to be. Thus the existence of God is not contingent, but a necessary existence. . . . The ground of His existence is within Himself, not outside Himself."[4] Thus Anselm, in His "ontological proof," argued God's existence from His essence. God is not only the ground of being, as Paul Tillich said, but He is Being itself. Though it is difficult to conceptualize, Aquinas' idea that God is the "First Mover" or the "uncaused cause" is probably more accurate than the idea that He is self-caused. Rather than being caused, God simply *is*. He exists without having been caused. God's existence is self-explained only in the sense that the nature of His essence requires it. This makes His existence independent from all causes.

Self-fulfilled in Trinity

Not only is God independent in existence, but secondly He is independent in the area of His fulfillment. For His own fulfillment He needs no relationship outside Himself. No created order is necessary for His personal gratification, satisfaction, contentment or emotional completion. He is self-fulfilled.

A strong case can be made that the term "person" by appropriate definition implies incompleteness. An individual cannot stand *as person* alone. Personality is a relational idea. Human persons have always found their most fulfilling experiences in personal relationships. In this way they are replicas of God. People are social creatures as God is a social God. If God's fulfillment comes from interpersonal relationships, we would expect Him to be fulfilled outside Himself, in which case He would lose His independence. The problem is resolved, of course, in the Christian doctrine of the Trinity.

When Dante's character in *The Divine Comedy* got a glimpse of the Eternal Light, he saw the Trinity and said:

> Not that more than one single substance was
> Within the living Light I looked upon
> Which is forever what it was before,
> But . . .
> In the profound and deep subsistence of
> The lofty Light, three whirling gyres appeared
> Having three colors and one measurement;
> One from another seemed to be reflected. . . .[5]

Dante's metaphor of three gyrating circular colors subsisting in the Eternal Light depicts the three personalities within Godhood, each a reflection of the other with the same dimensions and the same basic appearance, yet each a separate color.

Traditional theologians, banking on the Athanasian Creed, have understood God to be both unity and diversity (both one and three). But avoiding logical contradictions, they have maintained that He is united and separate in different ways rather than in the same way. They have said He is one in substance and separate in persons. Important to His personhood, however, is another kind of oneness that has been generally recognized but not traditionally enunciated. Members of the Trinity are not only substantively one; they are also relationally one.

Any analogy would be inadequate, but the relational oneness of the Trinity might be illustrated by a counterpoint musical composition. Certain pieces of music are composed of four separate melodies—soprano, alto, tenor and bass. Each melody is composed of succeeding notes that have mechanical relationship with the other notes in the same melody. Yet each note in each melody is so perfectly harmonized with its counterpart note in the other three melodies that the four notes become one chord of perfect harmony. Then the four separate compositions of melody become one composition of harmony. In melody we have mechanical relationships of successive notes based on order and arrangement, but in harmony we have a simultaneous relationship of contemporary notes based on inner congeniality and affinity.

In the Trinity, as in counterpoint composition, we see oneness from separateness. Unity comes from diversity with inner relational qualities. It is a oneness of harmonious relationship.

The monotheism of Judaism and Islam view God as personal, but they have no apologia for understanding Him as intrinsically relational. Only Christian monotheistic Trinitarianism has the theological "apparatus" for understanding God as innately personal. In the Trinity, the Father, Son and Holy Spirit are interdependent for relational fulfillment. As a person, each is incomplete. The Father is Father *to the Son*; the Son is Son *to the Father*; the Holy Spirit is the Spirit *of God*. What they are *as persons* is what they are *in relation to the others*. Trinitarian members are not isolated individuals in a generic class of deities who decided to pool their resources into a single unit. That would be tritheism rather than Trinitarianism. In the Trinity, each One finds His personal completion within Trinitarian relationships, not outside the Trinity. So far as we know, God could be metaphysically independent as a single individual, but He is self-fulfilled only as relational Persons. The idea of divine Trinity is that of three separate Persons voluntarily locked into intimate relationships—perfect persons by virtue of perfect relationships.

Like all personal relationships that are meaningful, Trinitarian relationships are based on love. Each Person is perfectly transparent to the others, voluntarily so, with no secretiveness. Each "occupies" the others' personalities. Intimacy is intense and absolute! Separate persons have relational oneness. Cohesiveness for the oneness is love. Polytheism embraces the idea of separate divine beings, but its deities are independent of each other, nonrelational and competitive. Only in Christian Trinitarian monotheism do we have the notion of perfect relationship. Consequently, within the Trinity we see perfect interpersonal fulfillment. In this sense God does not need the world or human beings. He is independent.

Relating with the World

Recognizing God's independence, Thomas Aquinas wrote that "creatures are . . . related to God, whereas in God there is no relation to creatures, but a relation only in idea."[6] John Sanders interprets Augustine as saying that God has no "real relationship" with His creatures.[7] Openness theology defines prayer as "genuine dialogue" with God and claims that "traditional theology has had a difficult time allowing for such dialogue."[8] The idea is that God has a formal but not a personal relationship with His people, that He hears prayer much as an answering machine picks up voice mail and records it. This is more than we can expect from the Aristotelian God, but it is less than the Scripture depicts and less than Church doctrine has generally held. Extremists who may have subscribed to the view have done so on the premise of God's independence, but they have not spoken for mainstream theology.

A great many behavioral scientists have failed to distinguish between *need* and *desire*. Any kind of human drive, emotional or physical, is included in the category of needs. To these psychologists a desire by definition is a need. Similarly, some religionists have failed to realize that God may have legitimate desires beyond His needs, and those desires can extend beyond

Himself and depend on outside relationships for their satisfaction. Augustine seemed to recognize the difference between need and desire when he referred to God as "never in need, yet rejoicing in gains."[9] Having desires beyond His needs does not in any way violate the principle of self-fulfillment. God desires human relationships because He has chosen to love human beings. He does not wish to shut up His majesty within Himself; He wants to share His glory and grandeur with His creatures. But He does not need those relationships to make up any deficit in His own life or to complete any personal deficiency.

Several years ago Jurgen Moltmann produced a book that revived ecclesiastical interest in the Trinity, in which he emphasized the importance of prayer in the context of Trinitarian thought.[10]

Openness theology has done the contemporary Church a signal service by re-emphasizing God's personal relationality with humankind. Pinnock describes "a God who does not remain at a safe distance, worrying about his own honor," not "a solitary, domineering individual but the essence of loving community . . . the ultimate in community, mutuality and sharing . . . essentially relational, ecstatic and alive . . . internally social and self-sufficient." The world is "an ecosystem capable of echoing back the triune life of God . . . enacting on the finite level the relational movements that occur eternally in God."[11]

In human life, those persons who are already fulfilled can enter into human relationships for unselfish reasons. Other-centered rather than self-centered, they have no reason to be possessive. Because God has social fulfillment within the Trinity, He enters into human relationships with no self-need. Without self-centeredness, He can initiate love sacrificially with those who are less than lovely. For us, relating with Him is not forced or strained. It comes easily. His congenial relationship with the world is not from lack of Trinitarian relationships, not in spite of Trinitarian relationships, but because of Trinitarian relationships. It is a reflection of His intrinsic relationships within the Trinity. God is relational with the world because He is independently fulfilled. Jesus even asked the Father to include His followers in something comparable to Trinitarian fellowship: "As thou . . . art in me, and I in thee, that they also may be one in us" (John 17:21, KJV).

Like Trinitarian relationships, divine-human relationships are grounded in God's initiated love, and they vigorously grow with our reciprocal love. If a relationship is coerced, it is meaningless. If it is regimented by legalism, it is mechanical. If it is based on fear of reprisal, it is calculated for effect. If it is voluntary, it becomes an experience of fellowship.

This kind of relationship with God provides human fulfillment and personality completion above all human relationships. It rescues the notions of self-actualization and self-realization from the pop psychologists. God's personhood, perpetually replenished in the Trinity, replenishes our depleted human personhood with richness and refinement and fulfillment.

God's independence does not prevent His relating with us. Our dependence requires our relating with Him.

Chapter 12

Impassibility and Affectability

The Old Testament drama weaves together two major story lines into a complex plot depicting a divine-human relationship that is enchanting in its suspense. One story line is the moral and religious history of a variously rebellious and obedient people, and the other is the divine initiative and reaction to their vacillating propensities. Subplots include the human tension between conflicting desires to please themselves and to serve God, and the divine tension between His demands for righteousness and His desire to favor the people with His presence. Since God initiates the relationship, the Hebrew Scripture is primarily a story of the divine relationship with people and secondarily a story of their relationship with Him.

In His role, God is also depicted as reacting to their rebellion and responding to their devotion not only by His overt actions but also by His emotional reactions. When human wickedness spread, "the LORD . . . was grieved in His heart" (Genesis 6:6). When Saul sinned, "the LORD was grieved" (1 Samuel 15:35, NIV). God "delights" in His people (Psalms 18:19; 37:23; Isaiah 62:4), He "rejoice[s] over them" (Jeremiah 32:41), and He allows people to weary Him (Malachi 2:17). He "laughs" and "scoffs," and has "anger" and "fury" over human rebellion (Psalm 2:4-5). He has "lovingkindness and compassion" (103:4); He is "compassionate and gracious," "abounding in lovingkindness" (103:8), and "has compassion on those who fear Him" (103:13). For His people, God said, "My heart is turned over within Me, all my compassions are kindled" (Hosea 11:8).

A great deal has been said about the Old Testament God of anger and the New Testament God of love. But other than the demonstration of God's love at the cross, no New Testament line pictures a God of love any more than Old Testament lines like: "I have loved you with an everlasting love" (Jeremiah 31:3) and numerous lines throughout the Psalms that speak of God's "lovingkindness, compassion and tender mercies." And no Old Testament picture portrays God's anger like the New Testament description of those who cried to the mountains and rocks, "Fall on us and hide us from the presence of Him who sits on the throne, and from the wrath of the Lamb" (Revelation 6:16).

Other Views of God

While the Hebrew people were discovering a God who revealed Himself as one having a broad range of feeling, 800 miles farther west Greek philosophers were speculating on an immobile God who was stale and sterile, dull and inactive, apathetic toward human feeling and numb to human need. Deity was depersonalized. In early Greek philosophy, divinity was synonymous with origin, power and destiny. God was defined in terms of "world stuff," variously considered to be water (*Thales*), air (*Anaximenes*), seeds (*Anaxagoras*), atoms and vacuoles (*Democritus*), earth, air, fire and water (*Empedocles*). Instead of seeking a personal God, Hellenism looked for a perfect substance from which the world could be explained.

That pre-Socratic philosophy was modified a bit by Plato and Aristotle who allowed the literature of tragedy with its emphasis on personal gods to be incorporated into their systems. But to them the gods were subsidiary to "God-ness," and the personal element was secondary to their primary emphasis on God as ultimate reality. This ultimate reality by definition required perfection, which required immutability, which required God to be incapable of being affected by humankind.

Church fathers found scriptural support for the transcendence, immutability and eternality of God, concepts that were consonant with Greek thought. With the influence of Greek philosophy, some of the fathers could not resist deducing from God's transcendence and immutability the notion of divine impassibility—that God is so self-contained and independent that He cannot be emotionally affected by human beings. His perfect serenity cannot be interrupted by human insolence nor His tranquillity disrupted by human turbulence. Because passion implies emotional change, it must be considered a defect. Most Christian thinkers agreed that God had feelings within Himself, but many held that those feelings could not be affected by outside beings or conditions. Thus, from the standpoint of humankind, God was void of passion.

These views were maintained by Ignatius and Irenaeus. Origen of Alexandria and Tertullian of Carthage held that only Jesus in His humanity could suffer; God could not suffer. Even contemporary Christians assume that God the Creator-Father cannot suffer physical pain because He is not physical. Only Jesus suffered physical pain. That is based on the assumption that what we call physical pain is in fact physical. Though we call it physical pain, the pain is actually in the mind rather than the body. Surgeons slice through muscle and nerve, and patients never feel it so long as they are kept asleep. In their minds amputees feel "phantom pains" in limbs that are not there. Since all pain is in the mind, I should think that even experiencing what we call physical pain would not be impossible to God.

Some "impassibility" theologians explain away all biblical references to God's emotional reaction to humankind as anthropomorphic. The references were simply expressions of divine truth in terms of human feelings, and therefore not precisely accurate. Renowned theologian Stephen Charnock says, "Those expressions of joy" ascribed to God should mean that "if God were capable of our passions he would discover himself in such cases as we do."[1]

Others of them insist that references to God's love do not refer to any emotional ingredient in God, but rather to His disposition and action toward people. What the Bible calls God's love is what we today would call charity. It is God's willingness to help us, prompted only by His choice without any motivating feeling for us as His children. He "loves" us in the same way that a philanthropist contributes to a fund for poverty relief, or like an estranged father voluntarily pays child support for children for whom he feels no affinity. God "loves" without feeling.

Thus Augustine prayed, "Thou lovest, without passion."[2] Anselm said, "Thou art compassionate in terms of our experience, and not compassionate in terms of Thy being. . . . When Thou beholdest us in our wretchedness, we experience the effect of compassion, but Thou dost not experience the feeling."[3] Aquinas reflects Augustine when he says, "He loves without passion."[4] If God's love were reciprocal, it would mean an infinite God was affected by the finite, which would make Him less than infinite. He, therefore, would function only from initiated love, never reciprocal love. His love may mean something to us, but ours cannot mean anything to Him.

Somewhat Impassible

Lest we completely discredit the notion of impassibility, I

wish to point out some important considerations. First, there is a moral ingredient in God's love that transcends emotion. While love includes emotion, genuine love cannot be reduced to emotional feeling. The picture of love in much of the American movie industry is nothing more than sentimental slush. As a consequence we have a sensate culture whose search for love is limited to sentiment, with no moral element that would require commitment. When Jesus said, "Thou shalt love" (Matthew 22:37, 39, KJV), He gave love a moral definition, implying that loving is something one can morally choose to do. While admitting that love includes feeling, we would be amiss to prioritize the emotional element in God's love over the moral. Recognizing God's impassibility helps us avoid that mistake.

Second, there is a constancy to God's love that is not subject to outside manipulation. It comes from what God is rather than what people do. His love is poured out from His goodness rather than drawn out by human appeal. It is not an effect of human causes. The notion of impassibility protects God from being pushed around by wind gusts of feeling and put in a tailspin by convulsive tornadic emotions. There is a constancy to God's love that is not affected by human behavior. Even if no human person should reciprocate God's love, His initiating love remains the same. Thus His love, constant and reliable, remains consistently intact.

Third, love has a voluntary character that makes it worthwhile. If it is earned, it is meaningless. If it is forced, it loses its spontaneity. If it is required, it loses its value. God's impassibility guarantees that His love is unconditional, unearned, undeserved. It is something He chooses to do rather than something over which He has no control. God is not the helpless victim of a love that dominates Him. He is the voluntary victim of a love He chooses. In a God whose love is not caused by outside influences, we see voluntary love.

Affectable

Against the background of these three considerations, we can reconcile the notions of impassibility and affectablilty, both of which function harmoniously in God. The secret is found in a two-word modifying phrase: *without consent*. God is impassible without consent to be affected, but He is affectable with consent. The nature of love is to be affected by its object. To choose to love is to consent to be affected. So to choose to be affected does not invalidate the notion of impassibility if being affected is only by consent. God's creation has therefore not made Him emotionally inconstant.

By the ontological nature of His being, God is impassible, transcending His creation, retaining perfect tranquillity above a turbulent universe. By the moral nature of His love, however, God is voluntarily affectable. His tranquillity is not to be mistaken for inertia or idleness. God is not a celestial iceberg, untouched and unmoved by human beings. He is awake, not asleep; He is alert, not groggy; He is responsive, not impassive. Scripture depicts a God who has chosen to be affected by His subjects. He has laid His feelings bare, exposing a tenderness and sensitivity at the heart of divine consciousness. He has allowed His people to contribute to both His pleasure and His pain. In doing so, God exemplifies divine humility.

God's relational love for humankind is generated in the dynamo of the Trinity where love is both initiated and reciprocated in a relational oneness that is absolute. Over and again Jesus stated the love between Himself and the Father. "I love the Father" (John 14:31); "the Father has loved Me" (15:9); "I . . . abide in His love" (15:10). Jesus prayed, "Thou didst love Me before the foundation of the world" (17:24), and he spoke of "the love wherewith Thou didst love Me" (17:26). In initiated love the subject chooses to love its object, which then becomes the subject of reciprocal love. But the object of reciprocal love so inspires and precipitates love in the subject that the object actually becomes the subject of the love, being the source of its inspiration. Instead of a subject-object relationship, love in the Trinity becomes a subject-subject relationship—like Martin Buber's I-Thou rather than I-It—initiating love and reciprocating love both moving in both directions, intimate and intense!

From impassibility God initiates love and from affectability He reciprocates love. The quality of love in the Trinity is the prototype for the relational love He wishes to flow between Himself and His people.

Though at bottom love is the choice for a certain disposition rather than an emotion, it nevertheless includes a positive emotional element that is inexpressibly fulfilling. Love also entails the possibility of negative emotions that can burn with unthinkable pain. Love does not require the actuality of those negative emotions but it cannot avoid their possibility, because loving makes one vulnerable to the object of one's love. More often than not, divine impassibility has referred to those negative feelings which God allegedly could not have. But by choosing to love, God makes Himself vulnerable to at least three painful negative emotions.

Vicarious Pain

The first is vicarious pain. Hurting with the one who hurts is a part of loving. Sympathy and pity are included in love. Hebrews says, We have a high priest who can "sympathize with our weaknesses" (4:15).

Process theologian John Cobb says sympathetic love means "feeling the feelings of others." He says people feel more deeply with members of their own body. If one's hand hurts, he hurts. If her spouse hurts, she hurts. Since to Process theism the world is God's actuality, when people hurt He hurts.[5] Without identifying God with the world as Process does,

Openness insists that God is affected by the hurts and bruises of a broken world.

Someone says, "If God really loves me, why doesn't He get off His ivory throne, get involved in my problems, and show me His love?" The Christian answer is that is exactly what He is doing every day, communicated to us so tangibly by the incarnate Christ that we cannot miss it. He got His fingernails dirty, His back sore, His hands calloused in a carpenter's shop. He tasted the frustrations and temptations that we face (Hebrews 4:15). He became the voluntary victim of human sin, taking into His body the pain of injustice. In His death He identified with the sinner vicariously in the strongest sense of the term.

When we encounter difficulties, we are tempted to wonder whether God is "out to lunch." We tend to believe God loves us in good times and forgets us in hard times. But God has not isolated Himself from human experience to insulate Himself from human pain. God enters the arena of human suffering and makes it His own. We do not see Him on a throne but on a cross. In the rough-and-tumble of human life God is not indifferent to human pain. He is not aloof to our fragmented world with its hunger, loneliness, oppression and exploitation. Love makes Him hurt.

Even Trinitarian relationships were not exempt from this negative fallout of vulnerable love. In the Son's exacting, excruciating pain during the Passion, God in heaven was suffering vicariously. Richard Rice says, "Identifying God with Jesus leads ultimately to the conclusion that what Jesus experienced in the depths of his anguish was experienced by God himself."[6]

Divine Wrath

The second negative emotion to which God's love makes Him vulnerable is wrath. Moses said to Aaron, "Wrath has gone forth from the LORD" (Numbers 16:46). He said to Israel, "You provoked the LORD your God to wrath" (Deuteronomy 9:7). Ezra spoke of "the fierce anger of our God" (Ezra 10:14). John said, "The wrath of God abides on him" who disobeys (John 3:36). Similar passages run throughout the Christian Scriptures, the New Testament as well as the Old.

Biblical writers spoke of both God's love and His wrath in the strongest, most superlative terms. Popular opinion has difficulty reconciling the two ideas, because we thoughtlessly assume that love is opposite wrath and should be its best antidote.

Our problem comes from a failure to distinguish between unworthy and worthy wrath. We observe persons behaving insanely in uncontrolled fits of rage, and we do not wish to attribute to God the same kind of madness. Without much thought we define all anger in terms of its most violent expressions. We recognize varying degrees of its intensity without noting basic differences. What the two kinds of wrath have in common is provoked emotional reaction. One difference is that the person with unworthy wrath is controlled by the emotion while the other has the emotion under control. If God were driven by storm bursts of reaction, it would undermine the stability that we ascribe to God. We would spend our lives "tiptoeing through the tulips," like pagans placating Him with pacifiers.

Another difference is the ingredients of the two kinds of anger. The basic element of unworthy wrath is an offended selfhood, while that of worthy wrath is an offended principle. The first is unholy wrath and the second is righteous indignation. We consider self-centered anger to be evil, but the ability to become righteously indignant is a virtue. A person who has no emotional reaction to evil atrocities is considered lacking in moral aptitude. Standing passively on the sidelines while evil people perpetrate heinous crimes against innocent victims is not an exhibition of moral goodness. To confess God without acknowledging His wrath is to suggest He is ethically indifferent toward sin.

Contrary to popular opinion, anger is not the antithesis of love. Passive indifference to rejection is no indication of love. Indifference shows disinterest, which is opposite affection. The antithesis of love is indifference. Anger is its corollary. When the love is pure, the anger from abused love is righteous.

Wrath, whether holy or unholy, hurts the one who carries it more than the one to whom it is directed. And the greater the love, the greater the capacity for the pain of wrath. Anger hurts! It burns like fire! The degree of pain in divine wrath is only measured by God's immeasurable love. In loving humankind, God made Himself vulnerable to the pain of anger.

Rejected Love

The third negative emotion to which God by love is vulnerable is the hurt of disappointment. True love includes both self-giving and the desire for response. If it is all desire with no commitment, it is selfishness rather than love. If it is all commitment without soliciting response, it is weakness. Love with response is pure pleasure. Without response, love is pure pain.

Loving is dangerous activity. It makes one vulnerable to the pain of rejection. The most intense torment ever experienced may be the anguish of rejected love. Choosing to love is choosing to chance the most devastating liabilities. There is no way to love and play it safe. The more intense the feelings of love, the greater the pain of rejection.

God's love for us creatures and our rejection of that love met on God's heart and riveted a cross of pain. Calvary's cross was a tangible expression of a greater cross that burned its way into God's heart when we betrayed His love. Without overlooking the primary substitutional aspect of the atonement, we need to see also its revelational role. At the cross God was revealing His love by exposing His pain.

In loving the world, God took a monumental risk. Chancing rejection, He left His feelings unguarded. He did not play His hand close to His vest. Willing to be affected by human betrayal, He left His emotions unprotected. He placed His feelings in a position to be crucified. It was a daring love, a dangerous love, an unsparing love that could not be contained. When betrayed, it erupted in unmitigated pain.

When an impassible God chose to love beyond Himself, He volunteered to be affected by those who reject. The pain of rejection is an indication of the strength of His love.

Chapter 13

Object of Worship and Interactive Friend

After everything we know about God has been said, there remains one overshadowing adjective that must be applied. To us, God is unfathomably mysterious.

The apostle Paul said we are "stewards of the mysteries of God" (1 Corinthians 4:1). He spoke of the "knowledge of God's mystery" (Colossians 2:2). He said, "Great is the mystery of godliness" (1 Timothy 3:16).

Certainly the systematic study of God needs to be done. The deconstructionism of Post-liberal theology leaves our understanding of God with nothing more than a gaseous, vaporous concept. But studying God systematically entails a sobering danger. A lurking liability crouches behind our attempts to analyze God, to categorize His attributes, to pigeonhole our propositions about Him. When we think we have explained Him, He loses mystery. As soon as we think we "have a handle on" what He is like, He ceases to be awesome. Then He loses appeal as an object of worship.

Being awesomely mysterious, however, He breaks out of many of our little formulations. Our calculus formulas cannot contain Him. He is too big for our cognitive compartments. He is too bright for our eyes. His genius defies our score charts and graphs.

Seven hundred years ago Italy's Dante wrote:

> Eternal Light, in Thyself only dwelling
> . . . for Thou
> Alone dost understand Thyself and art
> Fully comprehended by Thyself alone![1]

Attempting to probe the divine mystery, we use our best, "hottest," strongest words, all of which are inadequate. His mystery includes such impenetrable ideas as splendor, wealth, pomp, regality, imperial majesty, immensity, magnificence, brightness, glory and other unimaginable concepts for which we have no language. Paul spoke of "the riches of the glory of this mystery" (Colossians 1:27).

This volume has attempted to depict the relational aspect of God without sacrificing His infinite mystery. Since in our minds the two are in tension, we are apt to emphasize the one at the cost of the other. It is difficult to conceive of an infinite deity stooping to relate with finite creatures. Thus we either position God beyond human reach, as "rigid" theologians have often done, or we reduce God to our level, as both classical Liberalism and Process theism have tended to do. The first fault positions God as a mysterious object of worship, divesting Him of relational qualities. The second accommodates our ability to relate with Him, sacrificing His mystery.

Contemporary Christian culture is more interested in appropriating God for human utility than in the experience of worship. This generation wants a user-friendly God. Consequently, in reading a volume such as this which emphasizes the relationality of God, we are inclined to overlook the mystery required for worship.

The practice of worship, however, is no less essential to

Christian experience than relating with God. The first is needed to refine and direct; the second to make relating with God meaningful. Without worship, the most powerful and intimate of all relationships becomes a horizontal buddy-buddy experience rather than a vertical human-divine relationship. Something of a holy fear or reticence should mark our approach to the terrifying presence of God. In a way, it is a territory beyond us, of which we are unworthy and for which we are ill-equipped. Though we are exhorted to "come boldly" (Hebrews 4:16, KJV) to the throne of grace, we are not expected to come flippantly.

Mystery is an indispensable element for the reverence required of genuine worship. We are drawn to God while at the same time shrinking from Him. Charmed by the mystery that shrouds without obscuring the brightness of His personality, we worship from soul-depth—then blush that we cannot worship more deeply.

What we do know about God is so enthralling that we long to explore the mystery further. The exploration may employ our energies throughout eternities to come. Each unfolding vista will open panoramic scenes in a colorful display of divine personality. With each discovery will come a deeper perception of areas yet unexplored. The process becomes one of unending gratification because the One we worship is inexhaustible! What we have learned from this book is only the beginning.

Notes

Introduction

[1] Here "Liberal" does not refer to a position on the liberal-conservative spectrum, but to the classical theology of Liberalism. I have capitalized the word to be consistent with my capitalization of "Process" and "Openness" throughout the book when referring to those theologies.

[2] A.W. Tozer, *The Knowledge of the Holy* (San Francisco: Harper & Row, 1961), 35.

[3] Clark Pinnock, ed., *The Openness of God: A Biblical Challenge to the Traditional Understanding of God* (Downers Grove, IL: InterVarsity Press, 1994), 10. Contributors include Richard Rice, John Sanders, Clark H. Pinnock, William Hasker and David Basinger.

Chapter 1

[1] See Francis Turretin, *Institutes of Elenctic Theology*, vols. 1 and 2 (Phillipsburg, NJ: Presbyterian and Reformed, 1994).

[2] See William Ames, *The Marrow of Theology* (Boston: Pilgrim Press, 1968).

[3] See John W. Beardslee, III, *Reformed Dogmatics* (Oxford: Oxford University Press, 1965), 19. See also H. Orton Wiley, *Christian Theology*, vol. 1 (Kansas City, MO: Beacon Hill, 1960), 85-86.

[4] John Greenleaf Whittier, "The Eternal Goodness," Milton Ellis, Louise Pound and George W. Spohn, eds., *The College Book of American Literature* (New York: American Book Co., 1939), 733.

[5] David B. Burrell, *Aquinas: God and Action* (Notre Dame, IN: University of Notre Dame Press, 1979), 36.

[6] Rice in *Openness*, 11-12.

[7] Ibid., passim.

[8] Pinnock, *Openness*, 124-125.

9 I am using the term "perfectly" amorally, as wholeness, completeness, 100 percent. Webster includes in its definition of "perfect": "complete, absolute, whole, entire." So I am saying God cannot be completely (absolutely, wholly, entirely) ignorant because He is complete (absolute, whole, entire) in knowledge.

10 Charles Hartshorne, *The Divine Relativity* (New Haven, CT.: Yale, 1948).

Chapter 2

1 Tryon Edwards, ed., *The New Dictionary of Thoughts* (New York: Standard Book Co., 1955), 220.

2 Norman L. Geisler, "Process Theology," Stanley N. Gundry and Alan F. Johnson, eds., *Tensions in Contemporary Theology* (Chicago: Moody, 1976), 258.

3 Augustine, *The City of God*, tr. Marcus Dods (New York: Random House, 1950), 350.

4 Thomas Aquinas, *Compendium in Theology*, tr. Cyril Vollert (St. Louis, MO: B. Herder, 1947), 13.

5 A.H. Strong, *Systematic Theology*, vol. 1 (Westwood, NJ: Revell, 1967), 276-277.

6 Tozer, *The Knowledge of the Holy*, 39-40.

7 Henry C. Thiessen, *Lectures in Systematic Theology* (Grand Rapids, MI: Eerdmans, 1979), 78-79.

8 Paul Tillich, *The Eternal Now* (New York: Charles Scribner's Sons, 1963).

9 Millard J. Erickson, *Introducing Christian Doctrine* (Grand Rapids, MI: Baker, 1992), 84.

10 *The Works of John Wesley*, 3rd ed., vol. 6 (Kansas City, MO: Beacon Hill, reprinted 1986), 230.

11 H. Orton Wiley, *Christian Theology*, vol. 1 (Kansas City, MO: Beacon Hill Press, 9th printing, 1960), 335.

12 Richard Watson, *Theological Institutes* (Nashville: The Methodist Episcopal Church, South, 1875), 202-203.

13 John Miley, *Systematic Theology*, vol. 1 (New York: Eaton and Mains, 1892), 215.

14 John B. Cobb, Jr., *God and the World* (Philadelphia: Westminster, 1969), 77.

[15] David H. Freedman, "Cosmic Time Travel," *Discover*, June 1989, 59-64.

[16] Hugh Ross, "Cosmology's Holy Grail," *Christianity Today*, December 12, 1994, 26.

Chapter 3

[1] John Sanders in *Openness*, 59ff.

[2] William Hasker in *Openness*, 128.

[3] Pinnock, *Openness*, 120.

[4] Hasker in *Openness*, 128.

[5] William Hasker, *Metaphysics: Constructing a World View* (Downers Grove, IL: InterVarsity Press, 1983), 55.

[6] Tozer, *The Knowledge of the Holy*, 26.

[7] Pinnock, *Openness*, 121.

[8] Hasker in *Openness*, 128.

[9] Pinnock in *Openness*, 111.

[10] Ibid., 120.

[11] Rice in *Openness*, 36.

Chapter 4

[1] Pinnock, *Openness*, 123-124.

[2] Hasker in *Openness*, 148.

[3] Basinger in *Openness*, 163.

[4] Watson, *Theological Institutes*, 210ff.

[5] Miley, *Systematic Theology*, vol. 1, p. 180ff.

[6] *Works of John Wesley*, vol. 6, p. 230.

[7] Strong, *Systematic Theology*, vol. 1, p. 284.

[8] Pinnock, *Openness*, 123.

[9] John Milton, *Paradise Lost*, Book 3, M.H. Abrams, ed., *The Norton Anthology of English Literature* (New York: W.W. Norton and Company, 1968), 645.

[10] Pinnock, *Openness*, 121.

[11] Hasker in *Openness*, 147.

[12] Thiessen, *Lectures*, 81-82.

[13] Hasker in *Openness*, 148. He gives the same deductive argument in his book, *Metaphysics: Constructing a World View* (Downers Grove, IL: InterVarsity Press, 1983), 52.

Chapter 5

[1] Pinnock, *Openness*, 113.

[2] Ibid., 125.

[3] See Gottfried Wilhelm von Leibnitz, *New Essays on the Understanding*, ed. Philip P. Wiener, Leibnitz Selections (New York: Charles Scribner's Sons, 1951), 376, 411.

[4] See Wiley, *Christian Theology*, vol. 1, pp. 358-359; See also Miley, *Systematic Theology*, vol. 1, p.180-181.

[5] Rice in *Openness*, 52.

[6] Pinnock, *Openness*, 118.

[7] Basinger in *Openness*, 165.

[8] One may ask, "What is the biblical justification for these conclusions?" In the previous chapter I have dealt with most, if not all, the prominent Scriptures concerning God's foreknowledge. In order of their appearance in the chapter, they are Romans 8:29 and 11:2; 1 Peter 1:2; Isaiah 41:21-23; Psalm 139:16; Isaiah 14:24, 37:26 and 46:9-11; Jeremiah 32:37-41; Psalm 33:11; Ephesians 1:4; 2 Timothy 1:9; Titus 1:2; Isaiah 42:9, 44:7-8 and all of chapter 53, 65:24; Daniel 2:28; Mark 14:30; and Revelation 13:8. Additionally, in this chapter I have dealt with Jeremiah 32:35; Psalm 88:5; Isaiah 43:25; Jeremiah 23:39 and 31:34; Hebrews 8:12; Genesis 9:15; Exodus 2:24; Psalm 105:8; Ezekiel 16:60; and Jonah 3:4, 9-10. Admittedly, most of this has not taken the prescribed form of an exegetical study (though some of it has been expositional), but the prescribed form does not generally and properly belong to this volume.

    My conclusions in this chapter about the "voluntary non-consciousness" or "selective consciousness" of God cannot be drawn explicitly from Scripture. I have shown, however, that these conclusions are consonant with both the "all-knowing" Scriptures and the "forgetting" Scriptures and that the conclusions make the two complementary rather than contradictory.

Chapter 6

[1] Adam Clarke, *Christian Theology* (Salem, OH: H.E. Schmul, 1967, originally published in 1835), 70, 72.

2 Aquinas, *Compendium in Theology*, 22.

3 Cobb, *God and the World*, 91.

4 Ibid., 89-90.

5 Pinnock, *Openness*, 113.

6 Ibid., 116.

7 Ibid., 125.

8 Miley, *Systematic Theology,* vol. 1, pp. 212-213. See also Wiley, *Christian Theology*, 353.

9 In Genesis (17:1, 28:3, 35:11, 43:14, et al.) God was referred to as Shaddai. Though some of the rabbis played around with the term a bit to broaden its interpretation in the Talmud to include the element of sufficiency, the Septuagint interpreted it to denote sheer power, without broadening the term to include a connotation of ability that we often attach to the English word "power." The New Testament term is *pantokrator* (2 Corinthians 6:18; Revelation 1:8, 4:8, 11:17, 15:3, 16:7, 16:14, 19:6, 19:15, 21:22), translated "almighty," "all-powerful" or "omnipotent," with an additional connotation of "governing power," but not used in a context requiring it to mean infinite ability.

10 Jon Tal Murphree, *A Loving God and a Suffering World* (Downers Grove, IL: InterVarsity, 1981), 27-33.

11 Strong, *Systematic Theology,* vol. 1, p. 287.

12 Ibid., 288.

13 Thiessen, *Lectures,* 82.

14 Pinnock, *Openness*, 114.

Chapter 7

1 John Calvin, *Institutes of the Christian Religion*, bk. 3, ch. 23, art. 2. John T. McNeill, ed., Ford Lewis Battles, tr. (Philadelphia: Westminster, 1960), 949.

2 Ames, *The Marrow of Theology*, 153.

3 Watson, *Theological Institutes*, 607.

4 *The Works of John Wesley*, vol. 10, p. 221.

5 Ibid., 363.

6 For further explanation see my book, *When God Says You're OK* (Downers Grove, IL: InterVarsity, 1975), chapter 7.

7 "Contra Gentes," *St. Thomas Aquinas: Theological Texts*, ed. and trans. Thomas Gilby (Durham, NC: Labyrinth, 1955), 158.

8 Pinnock, *Openness*, 115.

9 Rice in *Openness*, 38.

10 *Works of John Wesley*, vol. 10, p. 236.

11 Pinnock, *Openness*, 125.

Chapter 8

1 Aquinas, "Summa Theologica" in *Theological Texts*, 160.

2 Some hold that these verses refer only to the availability of redemptive information. This is a matter of hermeneutics beyond exegetical analysis. Paul's phrase, "the grace of God that brings salvation has appeared to all men," I interpret to mean much more than availability of information, for certainly that information has *not* appeared to all men. I believe that God's Spirit is attempting to motivate all people and I interpret the verse to include this element.

3 Milton, *Paradise Lost*, bk 1, p. 604.

4 See Murphree, *A Loving God and a Suffering World*.

5 Aquinas, "Summa Theologica" in *Theological Texts*, 100.

6 Rice in *Openness*, 15.

Chapter 9

1 "Process theism" is a phrase frequently used for Process theology's theology of God.

2 Alfred North Whitehead, *Process and Reality* (New York: Macmillan, 1929).

3 Hartshorne, *Divine Relativity*. See also Hartshorne, *The Logic of Perfection* (LaSalle, IL: Open Court, 1962).

4 John A.T. Robinson, *Honest to God* (Philadelphia: Westminster, 1963).

5 See Jurgen Moltmann, *The Theology of Hope*, tr. James W. Leitsch (New York: Harper and Row, 1967).

6 Strong, *Systematic Theology*, vol. 1, p. 279.

7 Wiley, *Christian Theology*, vol. 1, p. 339.

8 Erickson, *Introducing Christian Doctrine*, 84.

9 "Summa Theologica" in *Basic Writings of Saint Thomas Aquinas*, ed. Anton C. Pegis (New York: Random House, 1945), vol. 1, p. 63.

10 The notion of God's omnipresence expresses His immanent relationship with what He has created. Without the creation, there could be no such relationship. The word "omnipresence" is not in the Bible. It is a term theologians use to express God's biblically implied presence in space. This conclusion is not simply an opinion of mine, but has been generally held by reputable evangelical theologians who define space as a part of the created order, as I have done in earlier chapters.

Chapter 10

1 See Burrell, *Aquinas: God and Action*, 40.

2 Anselm, *Proslogium*, tr. S. N. Deane (LaSalle, IL: Open Court, 1903), 25.

3 See Whitehead, *Process and Reality*.

4 Cobb, *God and the World*, 70, 77-78.

5 "Summa Theologica" in *Basic Writings of Aquinas*, vol. 1, p. 70.

6 Schubert M. Ogden, "The Reality of God," Ewart H. Cousins, ed. *Process Theology* (New York: Newman Press, 1971), 122.

7 Rice in *Openness*, 47.

8 Ibid., 48-49.

9 Pinnock, *Openness*, 118.

10 Rice in *Openness*, 48.

11 *The Confessions of St. Augustine* (Grand Rapids, MI: Baker, 1977), 2.

12 Burrell, *Aquinas: God and Action,* 38.

13 "Exposition, Apostles' Creed" in Aquinas, *Theological Texts*, 172-173.

14 Watson, *Theological Institutes,* 227.

15 Strong, *Systematic Theology,* vol. 1, p. 258.

16 Miley, *Systematic Theology,* vol. 1, p. 221.

17 Thiessen, *Lectures,* 83.

18 Wiley, *Christian Theology*, vol. 1, p. 341.

19 Sanders in *Openness*, 80.

20 Hasker in *Openness*, 133.

21 Wiley, *Christian Theology*, vol. 1, p. 340.

Chapter 11

1 Tozer, *The Knowledge of the Holy*, 32.

2 Alfred North Whitehead, "God and the World," in Cousins, *Process Theology*, 93.

3 Ogden in *Process Theology*, 121ff.

4 Strong, *Systematic Theology*, vol. 1, pp. 257, 256.

5 Dante Alighieri, *The Divine Comedy*, Canto 33, tr. Thomas G. Bergin (New York: Meredith Publishing Company, 1955), 107-108.

6 "Summa Theologica" in *Basic Writings of Aquinas*, vol. 1, p. 124.

7 Sanders in *Openness*, 84.

8 Pinnock, *Openness*, 8.

9 *Confessions of St. Augustine*, 2.

10 Jurgen Moltmann, *The Trinity and the Kingdom* (New York: Harper and Row, 1981).

11 Pinnock, *Openness*, 102, 108-110.

Chapter 12

1 Stephen Charnock, *The Existence and Attributes of God* (Ann Arbor, MI: Cushing-Mallory, 1958), 126.

2 *Confessions of St. Augustine*, 2.

3 Anselm, *Proslogium*, 13.

4 "Summa Theologica" in *Basic Writings of Aquinas*, vol. 1, p. 216.

5 John B. Cobb, Jr. and David Ray Griffin, *Process Theology* (Philadelphia: Westminster, 1976), 44.

6 Rice in *Openness*, 46.

Chapter 13

1 Dante, *Divine Comedy*, 108.

Other books by Jon Tal Murphree

The Love Motive
A Loving God and a Suffering World
When God Says You're OK